David
Rieff

SIMON & SCHUSTER

The Exile

CUBA
IN THE HEART
OF MIAMI

New York London Toronto Sydney
Tokyo Singapore

SIMON & SCHUSTER
Simon & Schuster Building
Rockefeller Center
1230 Avenue of the Americas
New York, New York 10020

Designed by Deirdre C. Amthor

Manufactured in the United States of America

1   3   5   7   9   10   8   6   4   2

Library of Congress Cataloging-in-Publication Data
Rieff, David.
The exile : Cuba in the heart of Miami / David Rieff.
p.   cm.
Includes bibliographical references.
1. Miami (Fla.)—Social conditions.   2. Cuban Americans—Florida—
Miami.   I. Title.
F319.M6R537   1993
975.9′004687291—dc20   93-12141   CIP

ISBN: 0-671-77604-5

*For Joan Didion and John Gregory Dunne
and in memory of Nestor Almendros*

It is possible that there is no other
memory than the memory of wounds.
—*Czeslaw Milosz*

1

IT TAKES NO MORE than forty-five minutes to fly from the Miami International Airport to José Martí International on the southern outskirts of Havana. And between Pigeon Key, the last shard of U.S. territory on the flight plan, and the point where the surf begins to break along the shore of a beach on the north coast of Cuba, the transit is shorter still, about twelve minutes all told out over open water. But unlike most journeys of such brief duration—and it takes less time to travel from Miami to Havana than it does to get from there to Tallahassee, Florida's state capital, just as it is quicker to go from Miami to Havana than it is to fly from the Cuban capital east to the island's second city, Santiago—such a voyage is anything but routine. Once, perhaps, before Fidel Castro took power in 1959 and both Miami and Havana began to metamorphose into the cities they were to become, it may have been possible to travel innocently, or even automatically, across the Florida Strait. In the fifties, there was even a ferry that crossed regularly from the island to Key West; the *City of Havana,* they called it. But it stopped running in 1960, as hostility between the United States and Cuba began to flare. Thereafter, all movement between the two countries would become, in moral, psychological, and political terms, among the longest and costliest journeys in the world, no matter what it looked like on a map.

At check-in, going in either direction, there is, these days, an air of nervous expectation that is at once carnivalesque and solemn. People laugh for no reason, burst into floods of tears for no reason, and seem to oscillate between behaving with excessive, ostentatious politeness toward one another and falling into unaccountable spasms of irritability. In Cuba people have long since grown resigned to standing on line for nearly everything, so for them the experience of having to turn up some three hours or more before the flight to Miami is scheduled to leave does not seem so very different, in creatural terms anyway, from their daily routine of queuing for bread, or rum, or cigarettes. Most consider themselves lucky to get to go, and a few boring hours are a small price to pay for the privilege of travel that is denied to most ordinary Cubans. The one oddity that departing passengers often remark on is that since those not actually booked on a flight are barred from entering the terminal proper, the people leaving for Miami must say good-bye to the people seeing them off in the open air. And this is in marked contrast to their normal experience, which in the close-knit society that is Cuba today is of doing almost everything in groups—in family units, as part of a cohort of friends, or with co-workers. Instead, once the long good-byes have been said, all those kisses lavished, all those children hugged, all those manly *abrazos* exchanged, the travelers must complete their journey in an altogether unfamiliar isolation, as if they were convicts, or refugees, or, perhaps, middle-class North Americans. That isolation is made all the more acute by the sharp-elbowed, jammed, disorganized maze they encounter once inside the jerry-built departure hall at José Martí, a place where gate assignments are often misleading and where unfinished bits of wiring dangle from the drop ceiling like so many icicles.

In Miami, to be sure, there will be a horde of family members waiting. They will be there on the other side of the arrivals barrier with their tears, their baskets of food, and, often, their camcorders to record the arrival of relatives many have never laid eyes on before and even those whom they have, they as often as not remember far more dimly than they would care to admit. But that is Miami, the other side, and in the sweltering heat of the José Martí parking lot, or during the punitive bureaucratic rigmarole of the departure formalities inside the terminal, Miami quite properly seems a universe away.

If anything, though, the distance separating Miami and Havana appears still greater from a South Florida vantage point. Prosperous Miami Cubans, many of whom routinely use Miami International Airport for their business trips to New York and Washington as well as for their holiday outings to Orlando or Cancún, are, in contrast to their relatives on the island, rarely much given to waiting calmly on line for anything. Miami, particularly Cuban Miami, is an impatient place, a city where motorists routinely flout stop signs and red lights, and, even in residential neighborhoods, will surge angrily around a car they think is proceeding along too slowly. Some Miamians, particularly native-born Americans, black and white, who have seen their city transformed into something almost unrecognizable over the past thirty years by its burgeoning Cuban population, tend to attribute this to the vagaries of what they often refer to rather euphemistically as "the Latin temperament." For them this is no simple xenophobic gibe—though it is often that as well—since many Cuban-Americans in Miami also have a weakness for explicating practically every difference between themselves and their non-Cuban neighbors in terms of this Latin temperament, if not, more grandiosely still, in terms of something they call "the Cuban character."

There are a few wags who have suggested that the crucial reason for this staccato quality of Miami life has nothing to do with temperament, but rather with chemistry, and that the habit of so many Cuban-Americans, the men particularly, of halting several times a day at outdoor stands for infusions of *café cubano*—a mixture strong enough to jolt even the most tranquil of nervous systems—is really at the root of the frenetic style that most people who know it associate with the city. But whatever the cause, and whatever the explanation—flippant, resentful, or self-aggrandizing—Miami is certainly anything but a quiet place, its inhabitants anything but passive.

But nevertheless, Latin temperament or no Latin temperament, at Miami International those who wait to check in for the Havana flight do so with a phlegm that would do credit to any group of East Havana housewives gathering in the predawn light in some residential neighborhood like Vedado or El Cerro outside a shuttered *bodega* or at a streetcorner where a truck laden with yucca or potatoes from the countryside is rumored to be heading. Since the trips from Miami to Havana were resumed in the mid-nineteen-eighties, they have been scheduled for either six in the morning or midnight, so perhaps some of the dazed attitude the travelers exhibit can be attributed to simple sleep deprivation. The more important factor, though, is that on the subject of Cuba, these ostentatiously impatient people have learned, over the course of three decades and at an incalculable cost, to be patient.

And most would doubtless not have slept in any case, on the eve of their embarkation on a journey to that place that, in the case of younger Cuban-Americans, they have never seen, or, for those who left after the triumph of the revolution—those five words that one hears so often both in Miami and in Havana pronounced as if they were only one: *eltriunfodelarevolución*—they have never revisited. Throughout the nineteen-sixties and most of the seventies, it was, in any event, forbidden to the Cuban-Americans of *el exilio*, "the exile," to visit the island. For the revolutionaries, and, for that matter, in the eyes of many ordinary Cubans who had chosen to remain, the Miami community were traitors, people to be excoriated as *gusanos*, "worms," and shunned if ever they were encountered. Cubans continued, in numbers that varied according to the vagaries of Fidel Castro's wishes and the ebb and flow of diplomacy and geopolitics, to go into exile in Miami, but once they had left there was no question of their ever returning even in the most extraordinary of circumstances. And so, for decades, the Cubans of South Florida sat helplessly by while back on the island—which was to say a mere ninety miles from Key West; one hundred and forty from Miami—their parents fell ill or died, relatives married and divorced, careers were undertaken, succeeded at, abandoned, and children were born and grew into adulthood.

Then, in the late nineteen-seventies, there came a brief period of opening. Much to the outrage of some vocal segments of the Cuban exile community in Miami (that other great center of the Cuban diaspora in the United States, the area of northern New Jersey around Union City, had never been able to muster even the limited political influence in Washington that the Miami exiles had acquired), the Carter administration decided to undertake the first serious effort to introduce détente into U.S.-Cuban relations since Castro had nationalized American economic holdings on the island in 1961. One of the interlocutors the Americans turned to was a liberal Cuban exile banker in Miami, a certain Bernardo Benes. With U.S. approval, Benes traveled to Havana, initiating not only the desired intergovernmental contacts but also that process which would come to be referred to in Miami as *El Diálogo,* "the Dialogue," the first serious encounter between the Cubans of the exile and the Cubans of the revolution—*los de aquí y los de allá,* "those from here and those from there," as many people continue to describe themselves, the here and the there varying depending on which side of the Florida Strait they sat on—since the failure of exile arms at the Bay of Pigs invasion in 1961.

For an all-too-short moment, it became possible once more for ordinary Cuban exiles to visit the country of their birth. The "worms" began to return, transmogrified, in official Cuban government pronouncements, as "gutterflies." And for all their understandable fear and festering bitterness, many seized the opportunity, including my friends Raul and Ninon Rodriguez. They had each left Havana in 1959, when they were both eleven. At the height of the Dialogue, in 1980, they were able to return for a week and set eyes as adults on the city of their birth. But they would not return again until 1990 and 1991, when I accompanied them on two trips to Havana.

If it was an opening, it did not last long. Perhaps too many hopes were pinned on such a frail reed, but whatever was responsible for the collapse of the negotiations, the budding amity of 1979 was soon replaced by stalemate, and then, in the spring and summer of 1980, the crisis at the Peruvian embassy in Havana and the Mariel boatlift. Spontaneously, at least according to every account except that of the Cuban government itself, a group of Havana dissidents drove a truck onto the guarded grounds of the Peruvian embassy in the Miramar section of the city, leaped out, and demanded political asylum. In the fracas, though, one of the Cuban policemen on duty at the embassy gate was killed. The Cuban authorities blamed the asylum-seekers; the dissidents denied all responsibility. When the Peruvian authorities declined to turn the refugees out, Fidel Castro ordered that the remaining police detail be withdrawn. Between that order's promulgation, on the morning of April 4, 1980, and the following afternoon, ten thousand would-be refugees rushed from every neighborhood in Havana and claimed sanctuary in the extraterritorial haven that was the embassy grounds.

An initial period of confusion was soon followed by intense negotiations. During this time, as both the sanitary and the psychological conditions at the embassy deteriorated, the Castro regime organized huge demonstrations along Fifth Avenue, Miramar's main thoroughfare, and, incidentally, the place where Raul Rodriguez had been born. Tens of thousands of Cubans turned out (or were turned out; accounts differed) to reaffirm their loyalty to their government and to denounce as traitors those who were clamoring to leave. These *actos de repudio*, "acts of repudiation," as they were called, can still be apprehended in photographic vignette by anyone who chooses to visit a fine house on Fifth Avenue in Miramar that is now the home of the Museum of the People in Revolutionary Struggle and was formerly the embassy of the Republic of Peru to the Republic of Cuba. Having made its point, however, the Castro regime eventually decided to allow the refugees to proceed on to South Florida. The port of Mariel, on Cuba's north coast, was designated as the sole authorized departure point. Not that the Cuban government would provide transportation. But it did announce that the Miami exiles could, if they wished, come to Mariel in boats and collect this *escoria*, "this scum," as Havana's Radio Rebelde had it; that is to say, their relatives.

Miami Cubans responded instantly. But when their ill-assorted fleet of pleasure cruisers, fishing boats, ferries, and motor launches began to arrive in Mariel, it turned out that there was a wrinkle. Those who were waiting at dockside were not only people who had opposed the regime, or had seized the opportunity to be reunited with their kin in Miami, but also included an enormous number of lunatics, common criminals, and homosexuals (homosexuality being a crime in revolutionary Cuba and a disgrace in capitalist Miami). Castro had seized on the opportunity and all but emptied his prisons and his insane asylums. What had seemed at first like a triumph for Cuban Miami turned out to be a time bomb, delivered C.O.D. Before the boatlift had ended, 125,000 new Cuban refugees had ended up in a Miami that all but had a collective nervous breakdown in its wake.

It was a brilliant theatrical coup on Fidel Castro's part. Once again, he proved that he knew how to turn even the most discomfiting situations to his advantage; once again, he proved how gravely both Miami and Washington had underestimated him. Within the United States, the results were not long in coming. Humiliatingly outmaneuvered, the Carter administration was understandably in no mood to continue a dialogue with Havana in any form. As for the Miami Cubans, they were so busy trying to assimilate the new refugee population in their midst, one that was more gay, poorer, and more nonwhite than any preceding group of Cuban refugees to have arrived in South Florida, that any thought of returning to Cuba once again, even for a visit to close relatives, quickly became something of an abstraction. There was more than enough "Cubanity" to deal with at home in Miami. Moreover, Mariel not only strengthened this "Cubanity" of the exile by injecting so many unassimilated Cubans into the Miami mix but it also stiffened the political resolve of even those relatively liberal Cuban exiles who had been sympathetic toward some form of reconciliation with Castro. How could one treat with a regime that thought nothing of sending florid schizophrenics and violent criminals north alongside innocent refugees? To do so would be immoral.

In reality, there had probably never been an enormous amount of support in Miami for climbing down even partway from what, in exile circles, had come to be known as the "vertical" position of unbending opposition and resistance to the tyranny of Fidel

Castro. But now, the boatlift seemed to demonstrate that the hardest of the hard-liners had been correct all along. One of the more unpleasant aftershocks of Mariel in Cuban Miami was to render almost respectable the views of such groups as Alpha 66 and Omega 7—groups that, if not directly implicated, certainly saw nothing wrong with terrorist acts like the blowing up of a Cubana de Aviación airliner over Barbados in 1976, a deed that left everyone on board dead—and draw the general consensus of popular opinion in South Florida even further rightward than it had been before Mariel. Even in those Miami circles where people had most staunchly sympathized with the objectives of the Dialogue, there was the pervasive sense that now was not the best time to visit Cuba and that perhaps it might be better to wait, as Miami Cubans had been waiting for so long, for the overthrow of Fidel Castro, no matter how remote or improbable such an eventuality appeared to be in the fall and winter of 1981.

But even the most vertical of positions have a way of lapsing into other, more commodious postures. In 1986, quietly at first, the flights between Miami and Havana were resumed. This time, they were organized by a company called Marazul Charters, which, in turn, leased some rather superannuated aircraft belonging to Haiti Trans Air—it was the *second* airline of that republic—on a twice-weekly basis. Marazul itself was the creation of a man named Francisco Aruca, a former militant in an anti-Castro Catholic youth organization who had been imprisoned in La Cabaña prison in Havana in the early sixties, escaped (according to some, dressed as a child, in a crowd of wives leaving the jail grounds after a monthly family visit), and finally made his way to the United States thanks to the good offices of the Brazilian embassy, in which he had been granted asylum. Aruca had gone on to study at Georgetown University, working as a bellhop in a Washington hotel to stay afloat, and, before too long, immersed himself in Cuban exile politics.

Unlike those of most former Cuban political prisoners, whose views only hardened with exile, Aruca's positions had grown steadily more dovish and even sympathetic toward the revolution the longer he lived in the United States. In the mid-seventies, a magazine he helped to found in New York City, *Areito,* could be found preaching an embryonic form of the Dialogue that was to follow and even a broader accommodation between the exile and the Cuban revolution. Marazul itself was prospering thanks to the tours it organized of East bloc countries—the sorts of tours that before the collapse of the Communist world were to be found advertised in small, left-wing American magazines and usually involved cruises down the Volga River or a week in the Hungarian wine country. So few who knew of him were surprised, when, in the mid-eighties, the Cuban authorities decided to permit a resumption of the flights, that it was Aruca, now well established in the tourist business and living in suburban Washington, to whom they would have to turn.

These days, seven years after returning to Miami, seven years of combining business interest with political conviction and keeping a near monopoly on the transportation of Cuban exiles to and from the island, Aruca is, if anything, a more controversial figure than ever. To the standard insults on Spanish-language radio in Miami—"Communist," "homosexual," "*dialogero*" —has been added another: "*Aruqista.*" Aruca himself now has his own radio station, Radio Progreso, that on an AM band almost entirely given over to the most vertical of anti-Castro programming broadcasts the news from Radio Havana and flails away at the received opinions of *el exilio.* Paradoxically, however, the Miami-Havana flights themselves are not particularly controversial except among the hardest of hard-core militants. To the contrary, they have become almost as much a part of the landscape of exile in Miami as the feverish discussions about what will happen to the island after Castro falls, or the regular use of a telephone link through Canada (the Cuban government has refused so far to permit any upgrading of its telecommunications links with the United States until its dispute with ITT over the monies owed the multinational over the nationalization of its assets thirty years ago is resolved) that permits people in Miami to talk to their relatives in Havana.

As for the thrice-weekly scenes of departure at Miami International, these scarcely excite any comment at all either from passersby on the concourse where Marazul has its check-in counter, or from the airport's largely Cuban-American ground staff. For a Miami Cuban to visit Havana is a rarity nowadays, but it is hardly unknown. The clerks in drugstores and supermarkets all over Miami are used to people stocking up on everything from babies' shoes to Tampax. Drugstores stock small-sized containers of talc, shampoo, and hand cream, and family-sized packs of chewing gum—perfect for gifts to the large extended families waiting in Havana. And photo stores are accustomed to processing slides of these trips, often in many copies for giving away, after the traveler has returned from Cuba, for friends and family in Miami who have remained behind.

This commerce has simply become part of the background noise of daily life in South Florida. By the same token, the sight of a long line of mostly elderly Cubans clutching all manner of parcels really is far less remarkable—once the political objections have been overcome—than the spectacle of red-faced German tourists heading for their departure gate at Miami International, their arms straining to encompass bags of luridly wrapped souvenir citrus fruits, after having spent a week at their condominiums on Miami Beach, or of Central American immigrants shepherding their enormous, trailing families through the crowded terminal as they try to locate a bus that might conceivably take them into downtown Miami or out to the agricultural country around Homestead. In airports like Miami's, places that have become the fraught antechambers to the new Babel that is the United States on this, the eve of the millennium, the sight of some well-heeled folks waiting on a slow-moving check-in line is hardly the most piquant or exotic of the many curiosities on offer.

Which does not make these scenes of departure any less moving, or, by the same token, render them any less predictable and formalized. For what is most striking about the departure of Cuban-Americans for Havana is the choreographed quality of their leaving. Almost invariably, as befits a culture in which children still routinely live at home at least until they get married, and in which, in Miami just as much as if not, for all the overweening material prosperity, more so than in Havana, several generations will often take up residence within walking distance of one another's homes, solitary departures are all but unheard of. The salient difference between José Martí International and the Miami airport is not one of sentiment but rather one of access. In South Florida, the check-in lines are not restricted to those actually traveling and so move forward buttressed by massive auxiliaries of relatives and friends. The final good-byes are said only at the last security barrier, and, even after the departing traveler has wrenchingly moved out of view once and for all, those who have accompanied him or her to the airport often can be seen lingering aimlessly on the now empty concourse, to all appearances either unwilling or unable to head for the parking lot and full acknowledgment of that sense that the thread of their lives has suddenly been loosened.

In other words, for every actual departure of a member of the Miami exile for a week-long stay in Cuba, there are any number of fantasy departures, aborted departures, or botched departures on the part of those who, for whatever reason, have decided not to essay the trip south. And among these people who have made this difficult decision *not* to go, there is often the strong and pervasive sense that in some very basic way their lives are on hold until the others who have actually gone to Cuba are safely back home in Miami. This becomes clear when the traveler does return. He or she is greeted with a fervor that transcends all cultural, all "temperamental," questions of a special Cuban demonstrativeness or family closeness. At the arrivals area, it is common to hear as many questions about the returnee's well-being as it is to hear inquiries about loved ones still living on the island. "Are you all right?" those who have come to the airport keep repeating. Then, since, people return from these journeys as empty-handed as they departed overloaded with goods, the newly reunited groups bypass the baggage claim and head for the exits, with the travelers again and again being assured that there are sandwiches and cold drinks in the car and that, in any case, there is a big *lechón asado,* or a paella, or a *palomilla* steak, waiting back at the house—as if those who have just returned on the Marazul flight had been gone for a year and not seven short days.

Later, over coffee, or else at breakfast the next morning, the traveler is more than likely to be reproached. "When you left, I thought I would die, and while you were gone, I did die a little each day," a Cuban mother of a friend of mine told him the day after his return to Miami. They were sitting on the terrace of a private club off Key Biscayne, palm trees to their backs and the Atlantic before them—a setting so idyllic as to be barely credible. And yet her remark was much more than simple histrionic posing—the kind of reproach indulged in by Cuban mothers, who in Miami are often indistinguishable in terms of stereotypes from the Jewish matrons of Miami Beach. It was posing, and performance, of course, but only trivially. The anguish was real. Cuban Miami, for all its outward prosperity and jauntiness, is a city in pain, a place where the dead are never far from people's minds, and in which the past and the present are constantly being elided. Those remaining behind are, from this point of view at least, quite within their rights to be furious with those who visit Cuba and return. They have forced the issue.

For to contemplate return, for those who do not actually have the experience, is again to come face to face with the pain of exile, with a sharply refocused sense of lives, and homes, and youth, all gone forever, with the gnawing discomfort that goes with being an immigrant, no matter how privileged an immigrant, in America, and with the inexpressible, desolate sense all exiles the world over share of being at ease and at home nowhere on earth. Those who make the trip to Cuba at least have the consolation of experiencing the hard sense of the place's reality for themselves. The dream vanishes, at least during the seven days of the visit. But for their relatives who choose to remain behind in Miami, this ripping off of scabs formed over the decades of exile can seem like something close to agony.

Not that those who do go ever undertake the trip with equanimity. There are political scruples to be confronted and agonized over, the guilty sense, which has been so successfully drummed into the Miami exiles since the first of them arrived in 1959, that to spend even one dime in convertible currency in Cuba—despite the fact that any expenditure there is bound to be overwhelmingly on gifts and supplies for relatives who otherwise might literally have trouble surviving the latest round of austerity measures imposed on the island by the regime (''the special period in time of peace,'' Castro dubbed the belt-tightening of 1991; there was more to follow)—is, in the words of Jorge Mas Canosa, the leader of the largest and most intransigent of mainstream exile political groupings, the Cuban-American National Foundation, to ''prolong the agony of the Cuban people.'' And whatever people in Miami think of Mas Canosa, they know there is justice in the claim. The Cuban government does make money on the Marazul flights, which are priced at a punitively high rate; it does profit indirectly from the money and goods that the exiles bring with them, though perhaps no more so than the governments of bankrupt nations all over the world, from El Salvador to Serbia, which are simply more honest about their dependence on remittances from their citizens working and living in Los Angeles, Düsseldorf, or, indeed, Miami; and the gifts the exiles bring have the emollient effect of making the ordinary Cubans who receive them a little less dissatisfied, and, conceivably, that much less inclined to agitate for political and social change on the island. In Cuba, in the nineties, to play Santa Claus—one of the main roles of the returning exile—is, at the very least, to act as a double agent as far as the regime is concerned, just as it is an exercise in ambivalence for the exile.

But such objections are largely political, and, despite the highly politicized quality of life in Miami, the deepest anxieties most of those contemplating a trip to Cuba experience have far less to do with their ideological convictions and far more to do with the rawer, more primordial question of their fear, their great fear. For Cuban-Americans who want to visit Havana must travel not on their U.S. documents but on Cuban passports that are issued to them by the Cuban interests section in Washington after the applications are vetted in Havana. For many in Miami, this is the first actual contact with the Cuban authorities they have ever had. For others, the older people especially, it is sure to bring back stark, unreconciled memories of the humiliations they underwent heading the other way, north toward Florida and exile, at the hands of revolutionary justice and revolutionary bureaucracy. The United States government offers a blanket exemption to its travel ban on Cuba to anyone with family there. But, under Cuban law, only those who left the island for good before January 1, 1959, and those who were born in the United States, and are thus considered to be American tourists not Cuban exiles, are exempted from the requirement to submit to the authority of the Cuban state.

When the documents do not arrive from Washington, people despair. But when the gray Cuban passports finally do arrive in the mail in Miami, they are like live hand grenades. And more than one Cuban exile has spent more than one sleepless night in homes all over Cuban Miami—Southwest, Little Havana, Westchester, Kendall, and Coral Gables—staring fixedly at a blue U.S. passport and that gray Cuban one, not knowing what to do or feel, not knowing whether to go to Havana or cancel the trip and stay in a Miami that suddenly seems both more alien and more like home than it ever has before.

In the night, in quiet moments, or driving to work, the anxieties can mount and multiply. What if I'm arrested on a trumped-up charge, drugs, say, or even some technical currency violation? Sure, it has not happened often, but it has happened. You read about it in *The Miami Herald*; maybe you've signed a petition demanding the poor fool's release. Or what if the Cuban authorities simply decide that they won't let me leave on the return flight I've booked, that there is something wrong with these papers they've issued me—"A mere formality, you understand, *compañero* [*compañero*? Christ!], and one that shouldn't take longer than a couple of days to clear up." In Miami, half the people you see in restaurants like the Versailles, or the Málaga, or the Centro Vasco, have mobile phones. There are scarcely any phones that work in Havana. And what will anyone be able to do, who will even find out what's happened to me? The American interests section? That's a joke. They have been largely powerless when such incidents have occurred. As the sign the Cuban authorities have put up across from their building on the Havana seawall, the Malecón, puts it, "Yankees, we are not in the least bit afraid of you!'' And while of course they are—they would not have put up such a sign if they weren't—this does not mean that a diplomatic protest on behalf of some Cuban-American silly enough to have returned home—Daniel going back *into* the lion's den after he had been let out once—will be made with much conviction or listened to at the foreign ministry with much interest.

To undertake such a journey, then, is the biggest step that any exile can make. Small wonder that when the doors of the Haiti Trans Air Boeing actually are prized open after the bumpy landing at José Martí—the airport was known as Rancho Boyeros when most of the returning travelers last set foot there, in many cases to board the so-called Freedom Flights to their Miami exile—there is at first the predictable, impatient stampede toward the door, but then, as the travelers look down the old-fashioned metal gangway, down at the the armed policemen in their green forage caps and the man in the *guayabera* shirt with his clipboard, and, beyond them, at the battered British Leyland buses waiting to ferry them to the terminal, but, most crucially, down at *Cuba,* there is a noticeable pause, followed by a collective, audible intake of breath. And only a moment after that do the passengers begin to descend down the ramp and onto the soil of the country in which most were born and which many have neither seen for as much as thirty-three years nor forgotten for more than half a day during all the time that has intervened since.

2

WHETHER OR NOT they actually chose to return to Cuba on a visit—and for the moment the vast majority did not—and whether most Miami Cubans imagined that they in fact ever would return to the island to live, even after Fidel Castro finally passed from the scene, their anguished longings for their own, defunct Havana, and, more comprehensively, for what was called in the exile *la Cuba de ayer,* "the Cuba of yesterday," were the spiritual glue that bonded the Cubans of South Florida together. Such doleful coherence, though, had immensely complicated what had been, to begin with, a deeply ambivalent attitude toward the United States. For thirty-three years, these Cubans had lived lives of triumphant ambiguity. Unlike earlier successful immigrant groups in America, the Cubans had experienced little if any slackening off in their attachment to their island homeland. At the same time, they had been immensely successful in the United States, and if their hearts had not yet fused with it, their interests and, especially, their pocketbooks had.

Such contradictions were hardly surprising, however much the native-born in South Florida continued to be astonished by them. Those who had come to Miami from Havana were not the poorest but rather the most privileged portion of the Cuban population, and this alone was enough to set them apart from almost every other immigrant group to the United States since the time of the Quakers and the Unitarians. Moreover, these exiles had not crossed a wide ocean but a narrow strait, had not insinuated themselves in an already bustling metropolis like New York or Chicago but settled in a small, provincial city that was still on the cusp of the expansion that would make Miami one of the most important cities in the United States by the mid-nineteen-eighties. What was Miami and what was Havana were, in any case, not so easy to distinguish. The two cities enjoyed the same climate, the same vegetation, and, once the Cuban exiles had reached a critical mass of half a million people, the same population. The result was that, though Cubans had prospered in Miami—indeed, their success and that of the city were, as they were only too ready to point out to resentful native-born Floridians, all but inseparable—buried their parents in its cemeteries, and educated their children in its schools and universities, they continued to live, metaphorically at least, with their bags packed and a strong fantasy alive in their hearts of what they would do in Cuba and for Cuba when, at last, they were finally able to return.

The fact that such ideas were, for the moment at least, chimerical, and that just as with every passing year the Cuba of yesterday receded further so as the Miami Cubans became more and more vested in South Florida their prospects of pulling up stakes and going home was also diminishing with time, paradoxically had done little to lessen their authority. If anything, the opposition both of non-Cubans in South Florida and, more implacably, of the Castro regime itself had strengthened the Miami Cubans' passionate allegiance to the idea of return in much the same way that lovers who hold themselves aloof tend to fan the flames of desire in those they have captivated. And such analogies with the travails of the personal life were hard to avoid in Miami, in part because over the decades the facts of exile had become in most people's minds all but inseparable from the *wound* of exile.

Outsiders could only see the inconsistencies, and the elaboration of them was a frequent subject of conversation among Anglos and blacks if, but more usually when, the talk turned to Cuban Miami. "They want to have it both ways," a Miami Beach philanthropist once remarked to me, with that bitterness that is such a commonplace when non-Cubans pause to contemplate *el exilio*. "You're a writer, a professional outsider. To you, Miami is interesting. But we have to live here and the fact that the Cubans can't seem to decide who or what they are is incredibly troubling.

"If you say to them," he continued, " 'Look, you're Americans now,' they usually shake their heads condescendingly and reply, 'No, no, no, no, no'—'no's' seem to come in sets of five with them—'we never chose to come here to the United States. Fidel Castro expelled us, and we were forced to go into exile, forced to go to Miami. We are many things, including pro-American, but we are not Americans, not yet anyway. We won't even know what we are until things actually change in Cuba, until we have the possibility of going back. Once the exile is over, things will change, because we Cubans will finally have the freedom to make up our own minds about whether we want to be immigrants or go home.' "

As he spoke, this elderly Jewish businessman more and more seemed to incarnate the Cuban everyman, "Señor Fulano de Tal," as he is known in Cuban Spanish, whom he was representing. Then he paused, shrugged, and, for a moment, became himself again. But after a short time, my acquaintance went back into character. His voice began to rise, first as an echo of his own frustration, but then in an all-too-accurate mimicking of the hectic speech patterns Cuban-Americans tend to adopt when talking about *el tema*, "the theme," that catchall phrase that describes for Cuban Miami everything relating to the exile, to the possibility of change on the island, and to the role Cuban-Americans might play in it.

"So you say," he went on, " 'Okay, I get it, you're exiles. But in that case why don't you stop complaining about not being accepted in American society, or dwelling on the way you have been slighted by this civic leader or misrepresented in that story in *The Miami Herald,* or complaining that one downtown law firm is prejudiced against Cubans or that corporation is too soft on Fidel Castro!' " He laughed derisively. "That's the point when they usually climb even higher onto their soapboxes and retort: 'You Americans talk as if we were interlopers. Remember, if you can, that Miami was a village before we Cubans arrived here. If this city is anything, it is thanks to our sweat, our energy. So don't accuse us of meddling. We've earned the right to campaign for our interests, whether it's in terms of set-asides for Cuban-American contractors and architects, representation on corporate boards, or, yes, U.S.-Cuba relations.'

"The truth is," he concluded, "that my Cuban neighbors want to be like Russian émigrés in Paris in 1920 and like African-Americans or Jews in America today at the same time."

And in a sense, he was right. Cuban Miami did want it both ways. But how could it have been otherwise! How could they not have had this curious, almost dialectical relationship with their own identity in this Miami, on this ground that was botanically identical to that of Havana, and in this place they could feel superior to culturally—as cosmopolites, even in exile, always feel superior to the provincial city to which history has consigned them. Before the Cuban revolution, Havana had been the paradigm, not sleepy Miami, and the rich of South Florida had looked forward to their trips there, not just for sexual high jinks, but for culture, glamour, and even high fashion. Mitchell Wolfson, one of the leading members of this Anglo Miami oligarchy, recalls that in the fifties his mother had her dresses made in a shop in Havana, when she didn't go to Paris or New York, that is. During the same period, rich Cubans went to Key Biscayne or Miami Beach regularly, using these then fairly bucolic resorts like spas, places to go to recuperate from the rigors of the Havana social whirl. All one had to do was remember that the name of the ferry from Cuba to Key West had been the *City of Havana,* not the *City of Miami,* to understand the cultural pecking order that was in force in those days. Add to this the seemingly unquenchable fantasy of return, and the belief that, as long as Fidel Castro remained in power, the business between Cuba and its exile remained unfinished, and whatever distinctions it might have been rational to expect the Miami Cubans to draw among the wound, the wish, and the reality, or, for that matter, between what it was to be an exile and what it was to be an immigrant, drawing them came to seem the unlikeliest act of all for *el exilio* to perform. For to do so would have been, imaginatively at least, the grossest act of psychological self-mutilation. The contradictions were infinitely preferable.

And perhaps they were not quite so contradictory as they usually appeared to non-Cubans. Leaving aside the fact that the model of the successful immigrant group rapidly choosing to assimilate—give or take a few penumbral traces of discarded ethnicity, these being for the most part culinary—was one that no longer, in an age of multiculturalist pieties, particularly recommended itself to native-born Americans who were themselves busy recuperating the ethnic identities their parents or grandparents had discarded, assimilation and exile were ideas that simply did not mix. Exile and business success, yes, or exile and participation in the civic life of South Florida. But to assimilate was to accept that the exile was over, and, on a political level, that Fidel Castro had won. And this Cuban Miami gave no sign of being prepared to contemplate, let alone accept. For to have done so would have meant finally submitting to the proposition that the past thirty-three years in South Florida, the decades of wishing for return, of tasting it in one's dreams, and of struggling to pass along these longings to one's children, one's ever more Americanized children, had all been for naught. It would have meant saying not just that the exile was over—that would have been painful enough—but that there had never really been an exile except in the mind of Miami.

By comparison, the price of living in a certain state of contradiction seemed cheap. Not that most Cuban Miamians were prepared to accept such an imputation. When called upon to reply to the accusations made by native-born Floridians, their response was less to deliver themselves of a Whitmanesque "Do I contradict myself? Very well then I contradict myself" than to counterattack. As a Cuban-American banker named Luis Botifoll, who was famous in *el exilio* not only for having run the first Cuban-owned bank in the U.S., the Republic National Bank, but for his cultural and political activism both in Havana, where he had edited the newspaper *El Mundo*, and in Miami, put it to me, "It will always be difficult for you Americans to understand the realities as we Cubans in Miami see them. Immigrants want to assimilate because, by and large, they have brought with them unhappy memories of their native countries. But we don't have bad memories of Cuba. Before 1959, we did not think the U.S. was better. We thought *Cuba* was better. And most of us still do. It isn't that I am not grateful to the United States, or that I don't love the United States. I do. But even though this country has been very good to me, even after thirty-three years I don't feel comfortable here. And the reason is simple. I would rather be in Cuba.''

Botifoll was not alone. Among people of his generation, the hunger to return was as strong as ever. One could hear it expressed over the Spanish-language radio stations in the voices—some still sturdy, others enfeebled and quavering—of the old men who called in regularly to reminisce about the way life had been in Cuba before they had left, or to muse over the chances that they would ever return home. What was heartrending about these voices was not what they were arguing—is it the disembodied quality of a call-in show that encourages the extreme rhetoric one so often hears there?—but their plan. Really, all the callers could have reduced their sentences to one word, ''Cuba,'' and have repeated it over and over again. The meaning would have been clear. And it was clear, anyway. ''I'm seventy years old,'' one man confided, ''and all I want is to die in my country.'' ''My memories are like seed corn,'' said another, ''but after thirty-three years, I've eaten most of it, and the only question is whether I'll get to die happy, in Cuba, or as a broken man here in Miami with Cuba in my heart.'' ''I can almost no longer bear it,'' said a third. ''Every year, I think, 'This is the year we return,' every New Year, I think, 'This is the last one I shall have to spend in the United States,' and yet the years roll around and at my age I don't have many more left me.''

Such emotions, though more acute among the old, were hardly restricted to them. Middle-aged Cubans, people who had been brought to the United States as children, whose memories were of Miami, not Havana, and framed in English, not Spanish, shared their parents' and grandparents' passion for Cuba to a surprising degree. This was the group that so enervated non-Cubans in South Florida. Here they were, to all appearances the exemplification of immigrant success, comfortable in the world of business and the professions, and yet they still insisted that they were different, that they were not Americans, but exiles. And yet they lived American lives. Their children rooted for the Miami Heat basketball team and had posters of rock bands like Metallica in their suburban bedrooms. What was wrong with these people, why did they persist in clinging to their dreams of an island so many had never even seen?

And in truth, while there were what might be called "professional Cubans," people who ate, slept, and breathed exile politics, among this middle generation in Cuban Miami, most admitted to their interest in return only sheepishly. *El tema* was only rarely something that would be brought up over lunch. It came up haltingly, or had to be precipitated, like a chemical reaction, by a long boozy evening, or in the psychic deshabille that sometimes accompanies breakfast early on a Sunday morning, or during a long drive. But once the subject was broached, it was like a dam bursting. What yearning for Cuba was exposed in those moments, and what discomfort with the present, the exile's American present. Such conversations might, indeed, have been about emotions, not realities—on a rational level, after all, most younger Cubans were pessimistic about the practicability of their returning to Cuba, even assuming that the Castro regime eventually collapsed—but, if anything, this made them more rather than less bemusing.

To be sure, the emotion was overlayed with irony. There is a running joke in Cuban Miami about the sort of exile who insists that everything was better in Cuba, and people laugh about Fulana de Tal, who, on a hot day in Miami, insists that in Havana (where, in fact the climate is identical) it was never this hot, and that "there were always breezes," or Fulano de Tal, who sits in a restaurant eating a salad, and suddenly looks up and says, "This is a sweet-tasting tomato, but you know, they were always juicier in Cuba." And yet the ability to see through such sentimental affectations of exile does not mean that the longings of

Cuban Miami are any less intense. On New Year's Eve of 1991, I joined Raul and Ninon Rodriguez for dinner at a new Italian restaurant in Coral Gables. Our host was Raul Masvidal. Masvidal had been prominent in Miami business and political circles during the seventies and eighties. The son of a Cuban senator of the pre-Castro period, Masvidal had run unsuccessfully for mayor of Miami, helped found the Cuban-American National Foundation, and started a profitable small bank. In the late eighties, things had turned sour for him. The Miami regional economy had moved from boom to bust, and his bank had been declared insolvent and taken over by the federal government. At the same time, Jorge Mas Canosa had consolidated his control over the Foundation and forced out his original collaborators, including Masvidal. These days, Masvidal was dividing his time between Miami and Puerto Rico, where, with a European partner, he had bought a farm that grew exotic peppers and sold them in Holland and Germany. Nonetheless, for a man for whom the last several years had been something of a siege, Masvidal gave nothing away. He was a perfect host, and, before we knew it, midnight was upon us.

As the band played, everyone at the table embraced. Then Masvidal raised his glass and offered what has been the signature phrase of Cuban Miami. "Next year in Havana," he said, and we all drank down the champagne and embraced again. "Next year in Havana," we all repeated solemnly. An older man might have left it there, as might a less intelligent one. But if Masvidal loved Cuba, and dreamed of return, he was also a realist. He signaled to the waiter to refill our glasses, and then, staring absently down at the table, murmured, "The first time I made that toast, I was still drinking milk with my dinner."

One could trace the rise and fall of the exile's hopes through the various slogans that had been coined over the years heralding the imminence of return, slogans proudly proclaimed, then quietly, downheartedly abandoned. *En el noventa, Fidel revienta*, "In 1990, Fidel will take off," was the legend on a T-shirt sold in shops all over Cuban Miami during that year. To encounter a stack of these shirts, not in a novelty shop or five-and-dime but a fashionable Cuban tailor's specializing in custom-made *guayabera* shirts and thousand-dollar linen suits, was to get the impression that belief in Castro's imminent departure was especially strong at that moment. In fact, however, every year since the mid-eighties entrepreneurs had sold a T-shirt stenciled with that year's numerals and the phrase "This year in a free Cuba." There were even ironists who collected them, claiming that a complete set would be valuable one day. A Cuban-American doctor who lived down the street from Raul and Ninon Rodriguez could be seen, on alternate days, jogging in a University of Miami T-shirt and the 1989 "free Cuba" one. Near the Coral Gables bungalow that I rented during my stay in Miami in 1991 and 1992, I used to encounter a young man who would walk his fierce-looking rottweiler wearing either the 1990 or 1991 version, the sleeves of which he had cut off, the better to exhibit his impressively muscular upper arms.

There was, of course, the annual problem of squaring this year's optimism with last year's disappointment, for to commission a new T-shirt inevitably meant consigning the previous model to a Bermuda triangle of lost illusions. At the Sastrería Ramon Puig, the *guayabera* shop where I first encountered the shirts, the matronly clerk behind the counter wrapped the two I bought with a wistful smile. "Let it come true this year," she said as she handed me an incongruous package containing one grand white linen *guayabera* and two ten-dollar T-shirts. But she did not sound persuaded. And oddly enough, it was President George Bush who best coped with this problem of squaring hope and prudence. During his 1992 commencement address to the graduating seniors of Florida International University, the president used one of the slogans, but incorporated one salient alteration. "*En los noventa, Fidel revienta,*" he declared in ringing tones, but by substituting that plural *los* for the singular *el,* he had turned the phrase so that it meant "During the nineties, Fidel will take off," which seemed like a safe bet given the news reports of economic deterioration on the island.

Or perhaps it was only a good bet, not a sure one. When the Soviet Union collapsed, many Cuban Miamians were quick to assume that Fidel Castro would soon follow his counterparts—the Czech Jakes, the Romanian Ceauşescu, and the German Honecker—into political and possibly literal oblivion. The little broadsheets that are distributed free along Miami's Eighth Street, the sentimental if no longer the actual heart of *el exilio* (in recent years, the Cubans have moved to the suburbs, and what is still called Little Havana is now largely Nicaraguan), trumpeted headlines that read, "It's Over" and "We've Won." Meanwhile, on the radio stations, excited voices talked increasingly about what the future would be like in a post-Communist Cuba, and debated the terms of the country's economic and social transformation. But by the summer of 1992, it had become clear that the Cuban revolution was a far hardier growth than its Eastern European cousins. Despite the withdrawal of Soviet aid, and the Cuban government's own proclamation of unparalleled austerity measures—"the special period in time of peace" was the phrase used by the authorities, though what they meant was war footing without a war—the regime defied those who had written its obituary and held on. Before too long, those triumphalist bumper stickers that had been all the rage in Cuban Miami in the wake of the defeat of the Sandinistas in Nicaragua and the U.S. invasion of Panama, and had read, "Daniel yesterday, Manuel today, Fidel tomorrow," suddenly seemed like curiosities of a happier time, symbols of one more dashed exile hope. The change might not take place next year, let alone tomorrow, after all.

But rather than lead Cuban Miami, however unhappily, toward more assimilation into what remained of an American mainstream, this fresh disappointment only heightened their sense of being out of place. Having suppressed their hopes (as opposed to their longings) of return during most of their exile, from 1961 when the anti-Castro invasion failed to the fall of the Berlin Wall in 1989, Cuban Miamians had allowed themselves to believe during 1990 and 1991 that change on the island was not only inevitable but forthcoming. But it had not come, and by 1993 they were being forced to think again, this time in an atmosphere of uncertainty that was, paradoxically, far more distressing than the atmosphere of hopelessness that had prevailed in the years before 1989. Despair was a known quantity, but to know that the Castro regime would fall someday but that this someday could be a decade on was almost unbearable. For it meant that while everything was psychically up for grabs, realistically all the cardinal points of the Cuban exile experience—whether with regard to Washington, South Florida, or Havana—had remained unchanged. And Miami seemed more like a halfway house than ever.

For the two years of enthusiastic belief in the imminent possibility of the end of the exile had led even that younger generation of Cuban-American adults who had considered themselves entirely Americanized, and who had, in numbers large enough to discomfit their more ethnically parochial elders, married non-Cubans—"He or she is married to an American" was the way such unions were all but universally described in Cuban Miami, which indicated a lot since both members of such couples were in fact likely to have been born in Dade County—and, when they spoke Spanish at all, did so mainly to their grandmothers, their usually Central American servants, or the Marielito waitresses in their favorite Cuban *cafeterías,* to once again become interested in Cuba. Raul Rodriguez's own kid brother, Frank, was a case in point. A successful lawyer who, in 1992, was in the process of setting up his own downtown firm, Frank Rodriguez tended to leave the room when he saw that the rest of an evening was going to be devoted to *el tema.* But as Raul liked to recount laughingly, there had come the day when he had been sitting in the offices of his own architectural firm in Coral Gables and Frank had called to bring the subject up himself. "Raul," he had blurted out, after the briefest of preambles, "how many square feet was our house in Miramar anyway?"

Nor was Frank Rodriguez exceptional in this rekindling of interest. Members of the dispossessed middle class, who had founded Cuban Miami, were bound to treat the prospect of returning to Cuba at least in part as an opportunity to regain the property they had lost, or, at a minimum, try to get some compensation for it. There were other material interests as well. The Miami Cubans had largely made their economic mark as entrepreneurs, so they were understandably tantalized, all questions of sentiment aside, by the notion that were they allowed to return to Cuba the possibility existed of making a financial killing. In the real world of Miami, as doubtless in most places, the distinction between *el tema,* which was always couched as an affair of patriotism, and of *el negocio,* "business," was scarcely as clear-cut as most people liked to pretend. And if the enthusiasm at this prospect of return had begun as an exultant expression of faith and political conviction, it had nonetheless soon spawned all sorts of business seminars, usually held at the better Miami hotels, in which sober-suited Cuban-American businessmen got briefings on the prospects for the Cuban economy in the post-Castro period, sector by promising sector.

On balance, however, it was still the dream of return, more than the lure of profits, that had set Miami on edge in a way it had not been since the early sixties. "You have to understand," Ninon Rodriguez had told me, when I was in Miami in the mid-eighties writing my first book about the city, "that this place is like Brigadoon. Everyone is dreaming here." Not for nothing was the finest novel by a member of the Anglophone younger generation of Cuban-American writers, Cristina Garcia, entitled *Dreaming in Cuban.* Of course, these dreams were almost uniformly dreams of yesterday and of tomorrow. For the most part, in spite of the steady movement of people north from Cuba to South Florida, *el exilio* almost seemed to prefer to remain somewhat hazy about the precise nature of present-day conditions on the island. Just as defining what it was to be Cuban in Miami in 1992 was psychologically dangerous, so defining what it was to be in Cuba in contemporary times was politically a risk. It was emblematic of the veil drawn over such matters that while *El Nuevo Herald,* the autonomous Spanish-language edition of *The Miami Herald,* which was directed almost entirely not at Spanish-speaking Miamians but at Cuban Miamians, ran a regular column about the Cuba of the fifties, and endless columns about what a post-Castro polity might look like, its editors knew better, from bitter experience, than to try to give a balanced view of what was going on in Cuba today.

To have done so would have meant risking being denounced as Castroites, or, at least, appeasers, not only by the Eighth Street radio jocks but by Jorge Mas Canosa's Cuban-American National Foundation. Indeed, in 1992, Mas Canosa launched a campaign of vilification against the *Herald,* comparing it—this was one of the more moderate calumnies—to *Granma,* organ of the Cuban Communist party. Later that year, the Foundation paid for advertisements that ran on Miami city buses and read, in English and in Spanish, "I don't believe *The Miami Herald.*" If the city was Brigadoon, it was a version of that mythic place where the dreaming was almost compulsory, or, at least, an act of will as much as bewitchment. And on the radio, there were those who came close to admitting this. As one talk show host put it, and she spoke for many, "I don't want pessimism, I want optimism. We're in a state of war, and I want Cubans in the exile to defend their rights in the exile and pursue the liberation of Cuba." In other words, to stop dreaming, or, in the case of the *Herald*'s unfavorable stories, to interrupt the dream, was itself a kind of undermining of the possibility of return. This was what non-Cuban Miamians missed when they talked about the drama between the Foundation and the *Herald* in terms of freedom of the press. It was not about reality—it was about dreams.

And the dreams of Miami had had their impact. Thirty-three years of talking about Cuba, thirty-three years of clinging to Miami as the one place where one could exist as an exile, rather than as an American (Cubans in New York or Los Angeles, where large communities existed, were thought by Miami Cubans to have lost much of their Cubanity), thirty-three years of eating, sleeping, and breathing *el tema,* had made some conversations impossible and others unavoidable. For a dream like the one *el exilio* had been dreaming is an unassailable emotion, and it was hardly surprising that over the decades Miami's attitude toward Havana and toward itself had been played out on this level in which feeling carried all before it. So many Miami Cubans simply loved Cuba—the Cuba of those dreams, that is—and the fact that this place no longer existed, that not only the island, but they themselves—the exiles—had evolved since 1959, was deemed to be irrelevant.

These exiles had carried Cuba with them on the ferries, on the rafts on which some of them had crossed the Florida Strait while others had died in the attempt, on the Freedom Flights, and during Mariel. Those who had stayed in Miami, and who had not moved on, into the present, into America, were not about to let it go. And not having to do so was the point of living in South Florida. It was a Miami boast that so many of the Cuban exiles who had first alighted in other parts of the world soon found themselves drawn, as if by some obscure law of magnetism, from Madrid, or New York, or London, to Miami, which is to say, to the closest version of Cuba that existed outside the island. And for those old enough to remember, there were ways in which the Miami of 1992 more closely resembled the Havana of 1958 than did contemporary Havana itself. Those who visited Cuba from Miami sometimes commented bitterly on this paradox. "When I went back to Havana in 1980," a friend of Raul and Ninon Rodriguez named Sandra Oldham told me one evening, "I ran into an old school friend, and the first thing I told her was 'I've returned home.' But the truth is that she herself immigrated to the States a few years later, and I remember that after a few months here in Miami, we got together and she said to me, 'Sandra, you were wrong. I'm the one who has come home to Cuba.' "

The irony was that Cubans who, in the nineteen-fifties, had inhabited one of the most cosmopolitan cities anywhere in the Americas had been decosmopolitanized in the course of their Miami exile. Its wound had reduced everything for them, narrowing their taste in food, in art, in manners. To be sure, this is an old immigrant story. What a shock it is, for example, for those used to the iconic parochialism of the American Irish, to visit Ireland and discover all sorts of habits of being and feeling rather than any one, generic "Irishness." But what has been a temptation for all immigrant groups in America—that is, the safety afforded by an intensified tribal solidarity—became a command for Cubans marked as much if not more by the injustice of their exile as by the inevitable travails of the immigrant. And since there was always the chance of returning, of righting the original wrong that expulsion had been in the first place, the need was pressing to keep Cubanness alive. At the same time, since all identity is fluid, not fixed, the only way to preserve community was to restrict it: geographically, to South Florida; culturally, to the cult of Cubanness; and psychically, to the myth of return. These were, of course, unconscious decisions; there was nothing to stop a Cuban-American with a yen to live in New York from doing so. And most Miami Cubans have not left, any more than most have given up their dream of someday returning to the island.

Throughout the nineteen-eighties and early nineties, despite the remarkable economic success of Cubans in the United States, and, for that matter, in other outposts of the Cuban diaspora like Puerto Rico, Venezuela, Mexico, and Spain, the traffic continued toward Miami rather than away from it. Recent arrivals might complain about the conformity there and mock *el exilio*'s more exaggerated pieties, but they came just the same. Knowing that the image Miami nurtured of Cuba was false obviously made life difficult for someone who had left the island in 1980 or 1985, like the columnist for *El Nuevo Herald* Jorge Davila, or for someone who had moved back to the city after a long stay in Madrid, like the talented young painter Arturo Rodriguez, but it seemed that the option of belonging to neither Cuban nation, not to Cuba and not to the exile, was even worse. And this too was hardly surprising. For all the talk in bourgeois living rooms all over the world of feeling at home everywhere, of being, as the cliché has it, "a citizen of the world," the ability to live comfortably without a motherland is a rare talent. For most people, no matter how emancipated from such vulgar feelings they imagine themselves to be, having no geographic "somewhere" to lay claim to is one of the most unsettling and unhappy destinies it is possible to experience. It is nothing less than moral homelessness, and few welcome it any more readily than a poor man welcomes the prospect of having to sleep in the street.

Jorge Davila described his own decision to move to Miami from Madrid, the city in which he had begun his exile, more in terms of its having mitigated the loss of Cuba than as a choice based on practical considerations. "It was difficult to get work in Spain, of course," he told me, "but really I came back to Miami

to be among Cubans and to be closer to Cuba." This explanation
he offered as if it were the most natural one in the world, and
there were nothing odd about his having exchanged a life in one
of the most interesting cities in the world for one in a place that,
whatever its promise, was nowhere near as exciting or, for all the
loose talk in Miami of the city being the capital of Latin America,
as important either economically or culturally. But for Davila,
whose heart was still in Havana, such considerations paled. If
Miami was the closest he could get to the island, Miami was
where he would go. It was more than a refuge, remaining, both
for those who lived there and for those on the island, a kind of
countermodel to the Cuba of the Castroite revolution. Miami,
said Davila, was after all a Cuban society in its own right, and a
successful one at that. Indeed, it was so successful that many
people in Havana, faced with the extraordinary privations of "the
special period in time of peace," consoled themselves with
dreams of their own, those of the material successes of their
relatives in Miami and of perhaps one day sharing in those successes.

Such weighty and conflicting expectations hardly made matters
any easier, either psychologically or politically, for those Miami
Cubans who dreamed either of returning to the island for good
after its putative social transformation or, more commonly, of
enjoying some sort of privileged access in a post-Castro Cuba of
the kind that diaspora Jews were at least pleased to imagine they
enjoyed in the state of Israel. Davila was particularly skeptical of
the efforts of people like Raul and Ninon Rodriguez, whom he
knew socially (Cuban Miami, capital of a diaspora though it may
be, is also a small town), to reconstitute a real connection between themselves and life on the island during the course of their
brief, if increasingly frequent, family visits. "Such trips are inevitably marked by three common features," he said: "nostalgia,
fear, and family obligation. Those who visit from Miami are
above all trying to recapture their pasts, in particular their childhoods. And as they do this, as they walk through the neighborhoods in which they were born, through Paseo, or El Cerro, or
Miramar, they are both exalted and filled with fear. This is not an

imagined fear; it's real enough. Because if they are afraid of the
State Security, or just the prospect of being used by the regime,
there is ample reason. State Security does know what they are
doing in Havana, and does track their movements. At times, it
will try to use them. It would be naive to think otherwise.

"Meanwhile," he continued, "there are the pressures from
family, big pressures. People go broke visiting Cuba, and certainly unless you're very rich it's always going to be a big financial problem. People's relatives and even people they meet
casually are constantly making all kinds of demands on the re-
turnees, and they in turn feel obliged to respond. Remember,
Cuban families are not like American ones. In Cuba, cousins are
like brothers. When I was finally let back in, I was asked to
arrange all sorts of problems. And I was glad to do it; I wanted
to. But it was still a lot to deal with, even for me, and unlike Raul
and Ninon, I didn't leave when I was still a child, and when Cuba
itself was a completely different kind of society. I am a child of
the system. I know how it works. And yet the prospect of return
still confuses and frightens me."

For Davila, the brief return visits the exiles undertook could
not possibly give them an accurate sense of what was going on in
Cuba. "To begin with, these trips are too short," he said—"only
a week. But the bigger problem, I think, is that they are too full
of feeling. People want to recapture everything, their entire pasts,
all at once. They already try to do this here in Miami. That's why
people who, if they lived in Spain, would smoke Marlboros or
some other international brand, here insist on smoking El Cuño,
a cigarette that reminds them of their fathers and even of their
grandfathers—which is to say, reminds them of their childhoods.
It's out of this same motivation that here in Miami you hear so
much Cuban music of the fifties among people who are too young
to have more than the vaguest direct memories of it themselves.
They were too young to dance to Benny Moré or make love with
Olga Guillot's songs on the record player. It was their parents
who had those experiences. But Benny Moré is still big here in
Miami, and even the cult of Santería is making a big comeback.
And the reason is that whether it's a crooner or some Babalawo

casting spells, these things all have the quality of an abstraction, the taste of forbidden fruit.

"Look," he said impatiently, "I've been through all these rituals myself, only from the Havana side, not the Miami side. They're mirror images, you know. When I lived in Havana, and thought, 'Whatever I do, I'll never get out of here,' I felt the same hunger for American rock music, in fact for everything American, that some exiles feel for all things Cuban. In those days, I wouldn't listen to anything else. Even now, try talking to a kid in Havana and interesting him in Benny Moré or the music of 'el feeling.' He'd hand you your head. And I understand what Raul and Ninon are going through. I stopped listening to rock when I came here to Miami. It doesn't interest me at all, and the thing is that I believe it would if I lived somewhere else, if this city didn't impose Cuba on you all the time."

The paradox was that it was actually far easier to get away from Cuba in Cuba itself than in Miami. On the island, the world of Benny Moré, and iconic national images like the red earth of Matanzas or the white sand of Varadero Beach, were only some of the images that furnished people's dreams. Most educated Cubans in Havana hungered for information about the rest of the world, and tended to grill visitors about the latest American pop stars or for descriptions of the most recent European films. But in Miami, from dawn to dusk, all people seemed to want to talk about was Cuba. "Moving here was like moving from one planet to another," a cinematographer called Carlos Chaviano confided to me one night, over dinner in Coral Gables. I expected him to say what an improvement life in Miami had been, but in fact what he felt was bewilderment, disappointment. "I imagined my colleagues would want to talk about Fellini or perhaps Gordon Willis. Instead, all I hear is about Cuban films, Cuban music, Cuban culture. It has been a great surprise."

Even Jorge Davila, whose writing was, after all, concerned with questions of Cuban politics and thus fit more comfortably into the mainstream of *el exilio,* conceded that he had been astonished, upon his arrival in Miami, by how imperiously faithful it had remained to these notions of Cubanness. This did not mean, he added quickly, that Miami's dreams and projections were accurate, but it did testify to their intensity and staying power. And though his decision to come to Miami showed that he too partook in *el exilio*'s communal obsessions, Davila had come to see one of his roles as a journalist as pouring cold water on these dreams. He seemed to enjoy puncturing a friend's oft-stated belief that the minute Castro left the scene the Cubans of the exile and the Cubans who had remained in Cuba would quickly discover how much they had in common, or pointing out to a Cuban millionaire acquaintance who insisted to him that the exile would provide the "patriotic capital" for Cuba's reconstruction that although investors might come up with some initial monies out of love for Cuba and in the first flush of the tyrant's downfall, thereafter they could be depended on to revert to the harder-headed denationalized calculus that they applied to all their other investments. Davila even said he doubted that the hunger so many Miami Cubans affected to feel for the island was entirely healthy, or that the sorrows of their lives could all be attributed to exile. "Your problems were not all created by geography and politics," he had told his idealistic friend, a former editorial writer for *The Miami Herald* named Sergio Lopéz-Miró. "They come from inside and you carry them with you wherever you go. Castro did not cause all the sufferings of people here in Miami, and what is worse, his fall will not resolve them all either."

But Davila readily conceded that even for him the line between dream and reality grew increasingly indistinct the longer he lived in Miami. He was a man who had lived the reality of Cuba, and he had left not because the regime had branded him an enemy but rather because he had chosen to oppose the regime. Indeed, before he became a dissident he had been the model of the revolutionary new man. Even over dinner in Miami, when he was reciting the checklist of his services to the revolution, he sounded like a choirboy reciting the litany or a page of *Granma* come to life. "As an adolescent, I did two literacy campaigns," he said. "I must have taught three peasants how to read. Because whatever they say here in Miami, those accomplishments were real. I worked on six sugar harvests, two coffee harvests, and I fought as a scout against the South Africans in Angola. My brother was killed there, in Africa. When people here were talking about Cuba, I was living it, living it as a hero. So I know, if anybody can know, just how different Cuba and the idea of Cuba people have here in Miami really are.''

And yet Davila shared Miami's longings, and waited, alongside the rest of *el exilio,* for the moment when he could return home. The decorated hero of revolutionary solidarity with Angola had sacrificed everything—his privileges, his work, his safety—to be allowed to leave Cuba with his family and what belongings they could carry with them. Now he longed for nothing more than to return. ''As things stand now, I could not go back,'' Davila said. ''But if Castro fell tomorrow, I think I would try to get back to Havana on the first available plane.''

''Are you really sure you would go back?'' I asked him.

Davila smiled. ''Well,'' he said, ''let's just say I hope and believe I would. But who can tell? Perhaps I have grown more used to this halfway house than I realize. I suspect that my wife already thinks rather differently. She would hear the news that everything had changed and immediately start asking the practical questions: 'How are we going to live if we return? Will we live as well in Havana as we do here in Miami? What about the children?' Good questions, if you see what I mean, the right questions.

''And you know,'' Jorge Davila said thoughtfully, looking down at his glass, ''I would be right but so would she.''

3

In his ability to differentiate between his passions and his common sense, his yearning to return to Havana and his suspicion that not only was he unlikely to get the chance any time soon but, if and when he did, it would probably not be on terms acceptable to the middle-class resident first of Madrid and lately of Miami that he had become, Jorge Davila was something of an exception by the standards of the exile. There were, of course, any number of Miami Cubans, especially among the cohorts under thirty, who disavowed any interest in becoming Cubans once again and whose interest in their own Cubanity was far more comprehensible as part of the contemporary American quest for ethnic roots than as a genuine identification with the idea of a second nationality. But among those who felt themselves drawn to the idea of themselves as exiles—a group whose number only seemed to grow as the prospect of radical change in Cuba loomed—there was a marked tendency to suppress exactly those doubts Davila had expressed, and, certainly, a reluctance to discuss them in front of outsiders, whether those outsiders were non-Cubans or Cuban-Americans with little taste for *el tema*. Besides, to talk of such contradictions was to speak in practical terms, and while Cuban Miami was hardheaded enough when it came to most topics, it took a dim view of skepticism where Cuba and return were concerned. Even Davila, for all his self-consciousness, appeared to want to ascribe the reservations he felt to his wife, as if apportioning the manly fervor to himself and the caution to her in a division of emotional labor that was bound to be familiar to those who knew that in traditional Cuban society the cliché was that women were simultaneously more timid and more practical than men.

For the most part, those who swore they would go back to the island the moment such a return became possible (and, in this, the men of *el exilio* were, indeed, far more likely to incline toward such categorical assertions than its women) did so in tones brimming with romance and fervor, a cast of speech that effectively manumitted those who employed it from the obligation of thinking with any other organ than their hearts. When taxed with this, many Miami Cubans were quite willing to admit that they were being unrealistic. "You're trying to get me to separate an emotional attachment, my hopes and dreams, from the reality of the situation," an official of the Miami Chamber of Commerce named Sandra Gonzalez-Levy once said to me with some asperity. "Maybe I'm not that mature. Maybe I can't. But then again, maybe I don't want to."

There was the crux of the matter. For while non-Cubans in South Florida, with their increasing sense of being outsiders in a place they once could call their own, onlookers in a family quarrel they only partly understood, might insist that the Cuban-American rejection of the relevance of reason to *el tema* proved the innate irrationality of Cuban political culture, the truth was that the exiles believed that any purely cerebral approach was entirely inappropriate. And however paradoxical such a stance might have seemed at first glance, there was in fact something entirely hardheaded, entirely, well, reasonable, about this reliance on feeling. It was the emotional reality of the exile, of the loss of Cuba and the inability to return, that kept Cuban-Americans involved. To talk about reason was to invoke notions of rational calculus, and by those standards absorption in the dramas of exile, at least for Cuban-Americans under forty and those who had been born in the United States, made little sense.

For by most objective criteria, the exiles probably should have concluded not simply that they were destined to remain in South Florida, but that they would be far better off if they did. That there were people in Cuban Miami who had been tortured, or had relatives still in Castro's jails, or had lost family to the revolution was a fact that neither could nor should have been ignored or forgiven. That most had lost property and status, and had been forced to start again in the inhospitable, alien context of the United States, a generation condemned to sacrificing themselves to regain for their children the middle-class comforts that should have been theirs as a birthright, neither could nor should have been forgotten. But while no tragedy can be quantified, even those Cubans absorbed by their own losses had to know some- where that their own tragedy paled with, say, that of the Euro- pean DPs at the end of the Second World War, the massacre of the East Timorese, or the fate of Colombia during "*la violen- cia,*" the civil war that had wracked that country during the forties and fifties. It was not that the sufferings of others should have consoled the exiles, any more than the admonition to "re- member the starving Armenians" consoled American children in the twenties and thirties who were loath to finish their dinners. Human beings are not made that way. But even in the ideological forcing house that is Cuban Miami, people are well aware—and if they are not, the headlines and the TV news are quick to inform them—that while they have their grievance and their pain, they live in a world awash in pain, and that, from Central America to Haiti, people are desperate to make their way to the Miami that the exile views with such mixed feelings.

And even in its grief and self-absorption, Cuban Miami was well aware of its accomplishments as well. The exiles had been successful. Certainly, the future of South Florida was unlikely to be as bright in the nineties as it had been in the boom years of the seventies and early eighties, when practically everything from small grocery stores to private banks had made money. Even those who were bullish about the economic prospects of post- Castro Cuba were usually willing to concede that the prospects for most people would always be better in the United States than on the island. Cuban Miamians had even discovered that certain American political trends like multiculturalism and affirmative action, which as people stuck on the political Right they mainly opposed, offered certain particular benefits to a community like theirs that was overwhelmingly white but also could, because of Hispanic surnames, be lumped in with other "minorities." Assuming they wanted to assume the motley of late-twentieth-century, hyphenated Americaness, it was hard to avoid concluding that the Cubans were well fixed in Miami.

But that was the point. So many of them did not want, or not yet anyway, to accept that they were in the United States for good. *El exilio* wanted to be just that, an exile, and it clung to that condition against all odds, defying demographic facts like intermarriage and cultural facts like the power of American consumer culture. Even the concession, readily obtainable in Miami, that those Cubans who left for other parts of the country were, in the main, "lost" to the community testified to the embattled quality of this self-definition. So did the admission of many people in their forties that their own sense of Cubanity was different from both that of their parents' generation and that of their children's. "It would be easier for me and my family," Raul Rodriguez told me one afternoon, as we drove toward his house on Sunset Drive, not far from the University of Miami campus he had attended as both an undergraduate and an architecture student, "if I could feel entirely Cuban, as people of Botifoll's age do, or entirely American, as my son, Ruly, does. But when the U.S. plays Cuba in some international sport, I don't know who to root for. It's like being the child of a messy divorce."

Rodriguez was a nonpolitical man, a person who construed the world largely in personal terms, and his desire simply for a reconciliation between Cubans, and, for that matter, between the country of his birth and the country in which he lived, made him an anomaly in the overheated, politicized atmosphere of the exile. But if what he did with his obsessions was exceptional, the nature of them was not. There were times when it could seem as if all of Cuban Miami was confronting the same demons, harvesting the same emotions, trying to cope with the same pain. Material satisfactions, the bourgeois privileges for which the first generation of exiles had strived so ardently, were not enough. For as Ninon Rodriguez liked to say, "there has to be some kind of closure, otherwise this story will go on and on, and we will never be at peace.''

This was the special Cuban story, the one that had drawn Jorge Davila back to Miami and dictated that the Rodriguezes, a cosmopolitan couple who had they not been absorbed in *el tema* would unquestionably have been more comfortable living in New York or Barcelona, remain there. But there were larger forces at work as well. For all that they denied it, the Miami Cuban middle class was prey to exactly the same obsessions and concerns as the American bourgeoisie as a whole. And not only self-described ''minorities''—blacks, ''Hispanics,'' and the rest—were increasingly interested in their ''roots'' (an interest that manifested itself in everything from the mounting prestige of ethnic studies courses in American universities, to freshly minted ethnic holidays like the mock-African Christmas replacement, Kwanzaa, to the more diffuse but also more pervasive insistence that the essence of the United States at the end of the twentieth century was not the old melting pot model of assimilation but multiculturalism), but white ethnic groups as well.

The attitude toward this ''hyphenating'' of the American experience was bound to be more ambivalent among whites, for whom the melting pot, at least as folk memory, was largely positive, than for nonwhite Americans, for whom it was not. But even among the Irish- and the Italian-Americans, two groups who had certainly ''melted,'' a new obsession with roots was hard to miss. A journalistic writer like Gay Talese, who had spent most of his career chronicling worlds outside the one in which he had grown up, suddenly turned his attention to his own background. He moved from writing about American sexual mores in *Thy Neighbor's Wife* to writing *Unto the Sons,* an account of his father's family in Italy and, later, of his own first-generation boyhood in the United States. The year before John Gregory Dunne had called his book of memoirs *Harp,* an allusion to the name his Irish forebears in Hartford, Connecticut, had been given by the WASP establishment of that city. And, of course, American Jews, from whom Miami Cubans had derived so many of their behavioral and political styles, remained obsessed not only with their own dramas of difference and assimilation but with another country, Israel, about which they harbored feelings only slightly less intense than those of *el exilio* for Cuba. If this kind of self-absorption was all right for the Jews of Miami Beach, more than one exile had been heard to ask plaintively, then why not for the Cubans of Kendall and Calle Ocho?

On reflection, it would have been more surprising had Cuban-Americans *not* been affected by this sea change in American attitudes toward ethnicity. Far from expressing, as non-Cuban Floridians liked to insist, some ethnic or national peculiarity, a tropism toward self-regard previously unheard of in America, the exile's concern with its own grievances and characteristics was paradoxical testimony to its assimilation to the national norm. Everywhere in the United States, reality was steadily ceding ground to feeling. "I don't say what I have written is *the* truth," Gay Talese insisted in an afterword to *Unto the Sons,* "but it is my truth." And that was the point that the exile had been making, in one form or another, ever since the first refugees were processed at the Freedom Tower in downtown Miami in 1959.

During the time I spent in Miami, Alex Haley, whose book *Roots* had presaged all these new American interests two decades before they really came to the fore, died of a heart attack in Seattle, Washington. As I read *Roots,* what seemed most striking and most peculiar was the degree to which Haley had felt free to re-create the world of Kunta Kinte, to claim simultaneously that he was writing truth, not fiction, but that where there were no documents he nonetheless felt free to imagine dialogue, thoughts, situations. In an afterword, after elaborating on all the copious research that he did before sitting down to write the book, Haley admits that "since I wasn't around when most of the story occurred, by far most of the dialogue and most of the incidents are of necessity a novelized amalgam of what I *know* took place together with what my researching led me to plausibly *feel* took place."

The italics are in the original. What was remarkable was how convinced Haley had been that, in the most essential sense, a feeling was a fact. Viewed from the perspective of Miami, such a conviction was the bedrock from which all the other assumptions about *el tema* sprung. People might disagree about what a post-Castro Cuba should look like. They most certainly did disagree about political strategy, since exile politics was, predictably enough, riven by faction and divided into any number of competing, often mutually antagonistic groupings. One could divide Miami into those who supported the Cuban-American National Foundation and those who did not, and, further, into those who had once supported it but couldn't stomach Jorge Mas Canosa's leadership and those who did not support it ever but who viewed it as a useful tool for pressuring the U.S. government. One could discern groups that supported tightening the embargo, groups that supported maintaining it, and even those few brave souls who clamored for its removal. Once could find liberals in the Cuban, pre-Castro sense, liberals in the American sense, Christian democrats, social democrats, even fascists. But all these competitors were as one where the question of their feeling for Cuba was concerned. And it was precisely that feeling, more than any particular set of political convictions, that lay at the core of even the bitterest disputes within the exile. There was a sense in which it was preferable to have a rancorous argument about Cuba than not to speak of *el tema* at all.

This did not mean that Jorge Mas Canosa of the Foundation and Carlos Alberto Montaner, the leader of a Madrid-based grouping of social democratic and Christian democratic parties called la Plataforma, "the Platform," did not in fact violently disagree nor that, in the event both continued to be politically active in a post-Castro Cuba, they would not continue to be enemies. But for the present, for as long as Fidel Castro remained in power in Havana, and the exile remained in Miami, all this talk was as much about its subtext—preserving the feeling for Cuba—as about its ostensible subject, return. What people wanted, of course, was for the pain and the loss to be assuaged. But given the choice between forgetting about Cuba and being in pain, the fallback position of the exile, after all its political disappointments, was, precisely, to make sure that the pain did not go away.

Realism did not come into it, not as long as Cuban Miamians could, just as Haley and Talese had done in other contexts, hew to "their" truth. It did not matter, nor did most pause to question, whether all this nostalgia, all these fantasies about *la Cuba de ayer,* really conformed to life on the island, even the life of the Havana middle and upper classes, before 1959. If anything, such specifics only got in the way of the feelings. If someone said, "I love Havana and I would prefer to live there instead of here in Miami," there was no argument. More concrete claims about the past were suspect, precisely because they, unlike expressions of deep emotion, were falsifiable. Indeed, intelligent Cuban-Americans were quick to lampoon those "professional" Cuban exiles who chose to claim that they had held some plum job, or kept a string of mistresses, or owned some vast agricultural holding, in prerevolutionary Cuba. "If all the people who claimed to have been sugar mill owners are telling the truth here in Miami, the only thing I can say is that Cuba must have shrunk since the revolution since it would have had to be the size of Brazil to accommodate all the properties people say they had," Raul Rodriguez once remarked to me, in what, for him, was an extremely caustic moment. Others, more comfortable with their cynicism, could go further. The Cuban-American journalist Luis Ortega talked of meeting people in Miami who were always complaining about their lost properties or boasting of their anti-Castro activities on the island, but who often turned out to have been peasants back home, or, for that matter, loyal servants of the regime who had, at one point or another, fallen out of favor with it.

It was not that these rewritings of one's material situation or ideological doings were any more extreme, as distortions went, than those idyllic tales so many Miami Cubans liked to spin about their blissful childhoods on the island. The salient difference, however, was that while false claims about one's own prosperity or one's parents' status were pretty universally condemned for the fantasies they were, many people in Miami were quick to insist that their own equally fantastic nostalgia for their childhoods needed to be evaluated according to entirely different criteria. Truth did not enter into what Sandra Gonzalez-Levy had called this "emotional attachment." And if such talk often called to mind Camus's quip that "the only paradises are those that are lost," it also went a long way toward explaining why so many Cubans, even after three generations, not only continued to live in South Florida, but, in many cases, were moving back to the region from other parts of the United States.

"I came back to Miami ten years ago to be closer to Cubans," a physician named Sandra Oldham told me one evening over dinner at Raul and Ninon Rodriguez's house. The three of them had been in a bilingual grammar school together in Havana in the fifties, had lost touch after the revolution, and had met up again in Miami, where, as adults, Raul and Ninon had fallen in love and married. "In Pittsburgh," Sandra continued, "there was almost no one who spoke Spanish and, in any case, I just never felt that Cubans were meant to live in snow. When they do, they somehow stop being Cubans in the same way. Here you have the same climate you had in Havana, and you have the coffee. Do you know Sarita at the Versailles? She makes the best cup of Cuban coffee in the city, which means, given the way things are on the island, probably the best cup in the world. You have the style, and the language."

All she had left out was the assertion that Havana had been more temperate because of its trade winds. But Sandra's nostalgia, it soon devolved, was less for the island as it now was than for her own Cuban past, for her childhood, and for the Miami she had pined for during the Pennsylvania winters. When I asked her whether it troubled her that the Cuba she treasured no longer existed in Cuba itself, up to and including the *café cubano,* which, as she was well aware, was all but unobtainable on the island, she shook her head emphatically. "I'm not talking about the island," she said. "In fact, although I might go back there to visit I have no illusions about returning there to live. My life is here in America. But in Miami, I can preserve and be close to so many of the things that belonged to the Cuba that I knew when I was growing up. That's very important to me. I'm a roots person, you see.

"People need roots," she continued, "or at least I do. In

Pittsburgh, the only Cubans I knew were myself and one other person. When I left, the Cuban population of Pittsburgh declined by fifty percent. And for me it wasn't a question of going somewhere like New York, or L.A., or even Philadelphia, where there are a lot of Spanish-speaking people; it was a question of my heritage, of my Cuban culture. I knew there were so many people here who shared the same past that I did. You know, I find myself in the ridiculous position of wanting to reassure you that some of my best friends are Americans, and that I love the United States. I *do* love it. But nobody outside of Miami could possibly understand what it was like to grow up in Havana in those days, or to have been a member of the Vedado Tennis Club, or to have gone to the Phillips School, the same school that Raul and Ninon and our other great friend, Waldo Reboredo—he's the only one of our group who remained in Cuba; I still don't know what became of him—attended. Here there are people within a four-block radius of this house who can understand perfectly what it was like for me, whose own memories complement mine.

"That's the point, you see. We all have these fractured, imperfect memories of what happened to us. It's not like that for you Americans. You can go back to your old grade school anytime you feel like it and say, 'That's where I used to play basketball,' or 'That's where I kissed a girl for the first time,' or whatever. But all this has been taken away from us, and, what's more, if we did go back, we would probably find everything so changed that we wouldn't find the landmarks of our youth. But here in Miami, we have each other. I have Raul and Ninon, and they have me. My hope is that together we can start figuring out what happened to us, start filling in the blanks."

Earlier in the evening, Raul, Ninon, and Sandra had all alluded at different moments to the "mystery" of their childhoods. "At the time," Raul said, "it seemed brutal. I couldn't understand why my parents had just taken me out of Havana. I'd been to Miami, of course, and my parents went there regularly. That's the way it was in those days, we all grew up in an environment where the United States was accessible, where you could go there to consume. But even after I was put on the ferry by my grandparents, my mother's parents, I didn't know why we were going. And for a while I thought we would all be going back. After all, it was September, and school would be starting soon. I was just looking forward to getting back and seeing my friends—remember, I was an eleven-year-old, and an overprotected eleven-year-old at that—to seeing Waldo, and Sandra, and Ninon. Instead, on September tenth—even today, after all these years, when that date rolls around, I get a terrible wrenching feeling in my gut—my dad took me for a walk on Miami Beach, near the apartment hotel where we had been staying, and told me that we couldn't go back to Havana and that he had enrolled me in Saint Patrick's School here in Miami.''

What Raul senior did not tell his son is that the reason the family could not return to the island was that he was implicated in anti-Castro plotting and that his financial involvement had been discovered. This was why Raul's parents, who had, ironically, been on holiday in Miami, had remained, and why they had sent for their children. But if the circumstances of the Rodriguez family's departure was special, political, in part because they were prominent, the owners of the Partagas cigarette company, one of the largest tobacco concerns on the island, this sense of being wrenched out of their lives was general to Cuban Miamians of Raul, Ninon, and Sandra's generation. Ninon's father, Frank Lavernia, had been a middle-class doctor, with no particular political interests, but he had acted just as decisively. Sandra's parents had done the same. And, their children told me, in the course of that long evening in Raul and Ninon Rodriguez's elegant, Cuban-style house in South Miami, they had never gotten over it. "We are all busy here solving the mystery," Sandra Oldham said, "the pain that those of us who against our will were forced to leave Cuba continue to feel."

"You talk as if you were kidnapped by your own parents," I said.

Sandra smiled. "Well, of course we weren't, but that is how it feels sometimes." She went on to reveal that she was a believer in those psychological explanations associated with the so-called recovery movement, and in particular with the writer and lecturer

John Bradshaw. "I believe," she said, "that within each of us there is an inner child and that until we address that child's wounds there is no moving on. The point of our trying to remember our childhoods, of paying attention to them, and grappling with the hurt we felt, is to come to some kind of resolution, not to wallow in our own misery. I know you don't believe in any of this, but I need to nurture and attend to that wounded Cuban eleven-year-old who didn't want to leave Cuba but was forced to because people were yelling at us in the street. I need to resolve the pain of the Cuban adolescent who felt completely out of place in an American school. Those kids there were light-years ahead of me in the way they dressed and thought. I was still playing with dolls; they were playing with boys.

"I remember the first day of school," she continued. "I came home to my father—and I knew perfectly well how little money we had, how difficult our circumstances had become in the United States—and I said, 'Dad, please, can you buy me a straight-cut dress? I don't think I'll survive if I have to go back to school dressed the way I was today.' And I suppose that although I have been successful and I have learned to work fanatically, American style, in the way people did not in the Havana of my girlhood, I feel most at home among people who share these feelings, who felt as out of place as I did, and, in some essential way, always will."

Raul and Ninon, for their part, were neither temperamentally nor intellectually drawn to the idea of explaining their discomfort or their sense of isolation in terms of some wounded inner child. While Sandra spoke glowingly of the recovery movement, they, in fact, shifted uncomfortably in their chairs. But whatever their reservations about this language, they too had the sense that what was necessary for Cuban Miamians like themselves was to confront what had happened in childhood, and, ideally at any rate, move beyond it stage by stage. For Sandra, that had meant moving to Miami. For Raul and Ninon, it had meant returning to Havana, first in 1980, and then in 1990 and 1991 on the trips on which I had accompanied them. "The more I go to Havana," Raul said, "the less I am the eleven-year-old I was when I left and the more I am able to behave as the person of forty-four that I am today. Things as simple as learning my way around the city, and as deep as meeting old friends and finding out what happened to each of us over the last thirty-three years, are part of this process.

"It's different for my mother's generation," he said. "They were adults in Havana. They enjoyed the city as adults, knew their way around, had lives there. And they knew why we were leaving. None of us did. Last week, I took my aunt and uncle to dinner. My mom was there, as were some friends of Ninon's father. And they were all talking about Havana geography. They would say, 'Do you remember where the old such-and-such bar was, or the barbershop on Obispo Street?' And I thought to myself, 'These are the same people who have given me such a hard time about making these trips to Havana. They can afford to: Their memories are firmly in place.' But for people of our generation, everything is a sort of blur. We were robbed of our mastery of our own city, a place we only got to know imperfectly, as children. So when I go back to Havana today, I'm starting to get all that back. I get to move in Havana as an adult. I get to find out where the streets lead to after all this time."

But the mystery was only part of it. While people like Raul had doubtless romanticized their own childhoods, the late fifties had, indeed, been a time of extraordinary prosperity and ease for the Cuban bourgeoisie—dream time just as much as a time to dream about. There was a photo of Raul and his friends, taken at the pool of his house in Miramar around 1955, that was so innocent, so cheerful, that it taxed credulity, just as, in retrospect, the life of the middle class in that time, in the United States just as much as in Cuba, taxed credulity. To look at Raul, at his brother Alex, and at their friends—Alberto Raurell, Jose Noval, Jorge Otero, Sixto Aquino, Alberto Otero, and Waldo Reboredo, all but the last of whom had been brought into exile by their parents after the triumph of the revolution—was to get a glimpse of a lost world that one would have had to have had a miserable childhood indeed not to yearn for. And many people now settling into middle age in Coral Gables, South Miami, and Kendall had photographs like the one Raul Rodriguez passed around that night, from his wife, to Sandra Oldham, to me, which, after we had looked at it, and they had commented excitedly, reminiscing about each of the boys in the picture, he held lightly in his big hands for a long time as we continued to talk.

What was difficult was to get anyone in middle-class Miami to admit that he or she had not been happy as a child. Even those who said they did not want to go back, like Sandra, or like Raul's partner in his architectural firm, Tony Quiroga, kept emphasizing how happy they had been, how this happiness had been taken away from them, but how its lingering trace in their memories was what made them absolutely refuse to give up their own sense of their Cubanity and their belief that they were exiles, at least until Castro fell and they could return if they wished. Indeed, when I was introduced to a man who did not share either this nostalgia or this sense of himself, Ninon Rodriguez would later tell me, as if by way of explanation, that he had been extremely unhappy as a child.

It was not simply that people like Raul or Tony Quiroga contrasted how hard they worked with the privileges of childhood. Work was different in the United States, they kept insisting, more brutal and demanding. There was a Cuban folk aphorism that Raul was fond of quoting that went, "Americans live to work, but Cubans work to live." And perhaps it was so in the fifties, a time when capitalism was not so demanding, nor were the prosperous bits of the Cuban economy especially hard-pressed by foreign competition. Raul's grandfather, who had emigrated from Asturias in northern Spain in 1919, part of the great early-twentieth-century movement of Spaniards to Cuba that had included Fidel Castro's father as well, had struggled. Neither Raul senior nor, obviously, his son had been obliged to, not until they had to flee to the United States, where, as Raul recalled, he and his seventy-year-old grandfather were, "together, one whole adult. I could speak English and get around; my grandfather was mature and had judgment."

But Raul Rodriguez had not wanted to become part of an adult; he had wanted, quite normally, to have the childhood that had begun in Miramar and been truncated not long after he got off the SS *City of Havana* in Key West, Florida, in 1959. And its loss almost seemed to blind people like Raul and Sandra to the possibility that their own sense of Cubanness might be purely generational, that it might stop with them. To be sure, they could talk about Cuba with their kids, or, as in Raul and Ninon's case, enroll their son Ruly in a bilingual magnet school and bring him with them on their trips to Havana. But how could the talk of even the most beloved and sensitive of parents compete with the blandishments of an entire culture, let alone that of an American popular culture that, so far, no society anywhere in the world—from Tientsin to Moscow—seemed strong enough or even inclined to resist?

These argonauts of nostalgia had American children. "In a way," Sandra Oldham admitted ruefully, "my daughter feels about Pittsburgh, where she lived until she was seven, the way that I feel about Havana, except that Pittsburgh wasn't taken away from her. Actually, the last time we were back, we visited our old house and got the people who live there now to let us look around. My daughter went upstairs to where her room had been, and suddenly I heard her shouting, 'Mom, Mom, they've cut the room in half.' So I rushed up, of course, but it was the same room. I had to tell her, 'No, Christine, they've just moved the furniture around.' And she kept saying, 'I remembered it as being so much bigger.' "

For Sandra herself, or Raul and Ninon for that matter, it was less a case of wanting to go back to see what size their rooms had actually been than of recapturing the feeling. And to do this, they resorted to talk, to contemplating artifacts of that time, like the photo Raul had passed around, but also to virtually provoking, as in a time-tested lab experiment, certain nostalgic reactions in themselves, whether by listening to the music of Benny Moré, or splashing their children with violet cologne—the smell of bourgeois schoolchildren in Havana before the revolution was available, again, in Cuban Miami, where the cologne was again being made—or smoking El Cuño cigarettes and drinking *café cubano* at some outdoor stand. And yet there was something troubling about these exercises, a willful self-diminishing as much as a self-realization that troubled me more and more the longer I remained in Miami.

It had been a long evening, and since all such conversations inevitably entail a good deal of distress for those answering questions like the ones I had been asking, and a predatory rudeness on the part of the writer, I brought up this desire to take refuge in Cuban middle-class folklore with more than a little anxiety. "What I don't understand," I said, "is why the things about Cuba that interest you not only are from the past—your past—but tend to be unimportant in any non-Cuban context. Look at Benny Moré. It's one thing to say that Benny Moré is a wonderful singer, or to listen to him to feel closer to Cuba, but to say, as Raul did earlier, and as I've heard many of you say, that Benny Moré was the greatest Cuban who ever lived is something else again. Imagine if you met a Dane and he said that the most important Dane who ever lived was not the philosopher Kierke-gaard, or the astronomer Tycho Brahe, or even Hans Christian Andersen, but the comedian Victor Borge. Now, arguably, Victor Borge *is* the most famous Dane in the world at the moment, but to take him as a model seems like an awfully modest ambition. Why not love Benny Moré's music, but aspire to something better?"

And the question did annoy Sandra Oldham, just as I had imagined it would. "That's just so American of you," she snapped. "You assume that technology is the best thing. You want us to want to be like Singapore, or maybe Israel. I know what you're talking about, because the part of me that is a medical doctor sympathizes with that view. But I don't want to be just a doctor. I want a heart as well as a brain, and not only does Benny Moré speak to the Cuban side of all of us here, I think he speaks to the part of us that is more worthwhile humanly."

Raul had been shaking his head. "I don't really see this the way either of you do," he said. "My personal opinion is that the reason Benny Moré is so central is that music is the one area of world culture that Cuba really did dominate for a while. The rhythm of the mambo was the rhythm of the planet during the fifties. Who are we supposed to use as role models? A fighter like Kid Chocolate? I don't want Ruly to be Kid Chocolate. A scientist like Carlos Finlay? Carlos Finlay was a great man, but Einstein was greater. But Benny Moré is in a class by himself. So when I listen to Benny Moré, I'm not just trying to get into a time capsule and head back for Havana circa 1957. What I'm doing is looking for something positive. Moré died in 1963, too early to take sides in the fight between the exile and the regime. We can all admire him, here and there. And maybe if we can agree to admire him, despite all the things that divide us, we can agree on other things as well.''

Raul was certainly right to insist on Moré's importance. But I still felt that there was something immensely frivolous, as well as immensely sad, about hoping that a pop singer's lyrics could effect the national reconciliation Raul so desperately wanted. Certainly, the respect accorded Moré would not have found favor with Raul and Ninon's parents' generation. Ninon had once told me that her father used to lecture her on not growing up to be a foolish, vain woman, and the word he had used to describe this condition was *mamboleta,* ''mambo dancer.'' But now, an exile community oriented toward hard work, study, moneymaking, and success filled its leisure hours with fantasies about the night-clubs of Havana in the late fifties. If they swayed to the mambo beat, or the crooning style that, in Cuba, had been called ''el feeling,'' this generation of hard-edged men and women in early middle age, the people who were taking over in South Florida, were again children, thrilling to the music their parents had danced to, the music of their golden, enchanted childhoods. And this gust of sound from the past provided a music balm for the wound that was exile.

''You really loved your childhoods,'' I said, rising to leave. As if in unison, Sandra, Raul, and Ninon all said, ''Yes, of course.'' ''It's not just a question of remembering the past through rose-colored glasses,'' Sandra said as she shook my hand. ''I remember thinking *at the time* how great things were, how special I felt.'' And both Raul and Ninon insisted they had felt the same way. As we walked out toward the cars, past the artfully illuminated tree ferns that surrounded the front of Raul's house, Ninon suddenly blurted out that she had suffered even more than either Raul or Sandra since she had been sent to school in the United States at the age of six because her parents wanted her to improve her English, returned a year later, and then been sent into exile four years after that. "I had two exiles," she said, a tremor in her voice. "I was sent away twice from the best place in the world."

Such are the wounds, unstanchable after three decades, of those who once felt themselves truly happy.

4

THE EXILE'S GRIEF for the Cuba that had been lost was an all but inescapable part of the ambient noise of Cuban Miami. For all its glittering appurtenances, its prosperity, and, at times, its self-satisfaction, there was a level on which no pleasure, no level of attainment, nor any material accumulation could make up for what had been taken away from these exiles by the triumph of Fidel Castro. Even people in Miami who were perfectly well aware that they had prospered in the United States to a degree that far outstripped anything they could have hoped for in a Cuba that had remained capitalist could not seem to shake their longing for what the revolution had denied them. The supermarkets of Coral Gables might burst with every imaginable product, but it was commonplace to hear Cuban housewives insist that in Havana the sugar had been sweeter, the mangoes fleshier, and the pork more succulent. And the fact that in Cuba, not *la Cuba de ayer* but the Cuba that actually was, sugar was rationed, mangoes hard to come by, and pork not the stuff that dreams were made of was little or no consolation.

Everyone knew on some level that this attitude was a conceit, but if it was this did not make it any less ingrained. Sophisticates and workmen from Hialeah were equally prey to it, and the table talk in good restaurants in Coral Gables was as likely to give rise to it as call-in shows on the Calle Ocho radio stations. I recall an evening in Miami when I went with a group of friends to try a new Portuguese restaurant called Old Lisbon that had just opened on Coral Way. We had scarcely been seated when the owner bustled over, greeting us first in Spanish and then in English, both of which he spoke fluently. One of the people I was with asked him what he had done before opening this place, and he replied that he had worked on cruise ships, and, after that, as the majordomo to an aristocratic Spanish lady who spent part of her year on Key Biscayne. He did not seem delighted by the thought of her, and only brightened when I asked him where he was from originally. "Madeira," he replied with a wide nostalgic smile, "home of the most beautiful beaches in the world."

With this rhetorical flourish, he left us. It was a small place and for a moment we all remained silent. Then, when the sound of his voice bellowing in Portuguese at the cook over some dereliction or other assured us that his attention was otherwise engaged, we began to laugh. I thought I knew why, but I didn't. I realized that when one of my companions took a sip of his *vinho verde* and blurted out, "Can you imagine? Who could really believe that the best beaches in the world are in the Azores? It's ridiculous."

We were back on *el tema,* although it took me another moment before I caught on. "Oh," I said, putting down my own glass. "You mean that the best beaches in the world aren't in Portugal, they're in Cuba, don't you?"

It was a belief that allowed for no compromise. "*Chico,*" this cosmopolitan advertising executive, who at drinks earlier in the evening had been discoursing knowledgeably on the differences between Barcelona and Madrid, told me earnestly, "I know they are. Everybody does. Varadero is simply the greatest beach in the world. You know the saying, I'm sure, that the sand there is so fine you can snort it. That place has to be something."

By this time, of course, he was partly joking, and we all laughed again—was it in a slightly uncomfortable, *pro forma* way, or is this my imagination?—and soon changed the subject. But the original impulse, or, rather, my companion's original eruption of feeling, since his remark had been completely spontaneous, was one that most Cuban Miamians would at least have recognized in themselves and of which many would have admitted themselves to be capable. My great lost beach, my great lost childhood, my great lost city. All of these assertions, whether they were delivered flippantly, as in this bit of predinner banter, or with the most passionate sincerity, amounted to the same incantatory summoning up of Cuba itself, the great lost country. It did not really matter what the ostensible topic of conversation was—rationally, after all, my companion would have been the first to concede the existence of other beaches as beautiful as Varadero—because what was ostensibly being discussed was not really the issue. A more taciturn culture than the Cuban might have simply uttered the two syllables "Cu-ba" and left it at that, but even in verbose Miami, the effect was more or less the same.

It was an exercise that depended, to a very large degree, on believing but not on knowing from firsthand experience, on imagining but on never having seen, and on myths handed down from generation to generation rather than on anything that could be verified by a disinterested outsider. It was a case of beauty—the beauty of Cuba, that is—being in the eye of the beholder. When my companion that night at dinner on Coral Way said of Varadero Beach that it *had* to be something, the verb he used was all too appropriate. Because the truth was that he had left Havana as a small child and, by his own admission, retained only the haziest memories of the summer holidays he had spent on that beach with his family. But in Miami, in exile, he had grown up with the myth of Varadero. Its image decorated the walls of a dozen cafeterias where he went for a quick pork sandwich, a *media-noche,* after a Hurricanes football game at the Orange Bowl, and was stuck, the vivid colors gradually fading as the celluloid aged, in any number of family albums that were likely to be brought out during gatherings where the subject turned, as it so often did, to the past and to the homeland.

Only those who had been to Cuba themselves on family unification visits of the kind Raul and Ninon Rodriguez had undertaken, or those who had arrived in Miami in the decade following the Mariel boatlift of 1980, could maintain any degree of skepticism or distance. In Raul and Ninon's case, this was because, whatever their hopes, they had seen for themselves what Cuba had become. For the more recent arrivals, Cuba was not an abstraction or a cause; it was a place, the place in which they had grown up. They might detest Communism as passionately as the most hard-line member of the Cuban-American National Foundation—indeed, the recent arrivals provided that group with many of its staunchest new recruits—but it was, until they got to Miami anyway, the only system they had ever known. The sweetness of Cuban life before the triumph of the revolution was as chimerical as life during the Spanish colony. The real sweetness of life was to be found in Cuban Miami, in this Cuba of yesterday that the exiles had managed to create and in the plethora of food and consumer goods that were available within it.

I once sat in on a class at Miami-Dade Community College in which the teacher, herself a Cuban-American, invited her mostly Cuban-American students to describe what they thought Cuba was like. There was, predictably, much talk of state repression and of the sufferings of their relatives. But when the conversation turned to Cuba's natural conditions, these wised-up, superficially rather cynical young people might as well have been describing a Garden of Eden. "My dad says he was so lucky to be born in Cuba," a blond boy in a pair of cutoffs and a Miami Hurricanes T-shirt said serenely. "He always told us that people there looked after one another, not like here." Another said, "The old folks all say it was great. I know that on hot days my mom is always complaining about having to stay indoors with the air conditioner. It was never that hot in Cuba, she says."

On and on they went, an anthology of all the clichés that *el exilio* was famous for. These were opinions lightly held, of course, as opinions are supposed to be in the United States these days, and it is quite possible that had their teacher been inclined to challenge these assumptions these kids would have backed away from them. As it happened, though, the challenge came from one of the two Marielitos in the class, who, for most of the discussion, had remained silent. Finally, one of them, a mulatto boy with a tiny goatee, and a strange, slightly melancholy expression, burst out in heavily accented English: "I think you're all nuts. You people in Miami all talk about Cuba this and Cuba that. Cuba was so great, you say. Everything was better there.

Well, what do you know about Cuba? Why don't you ask me about Cuba? You want to talk about breezes? Man, I never was hot in Miami like I was hot in Havana. You know why? Air-conditioning. I'd never seen an air conditioner until I came to this country. And Cuban food? The best Cuban food is here. In Havana, you're lucky just to get enough to eat, never mind what it tastes like. You're all like some guy who's in love with some girl who doesn't want nothing to do with him. You dream about her, and write her name down over and over again, and pretty soon you've made her up, 'cause she's nothing like what you imagine. Well, I'm here to tell you, neither is Cuba!''

There was an embarrassed silence. The blond boy, who had been doodling in his notebook during his classmate's tirade, looked up and said, "Juan, brother, we hear you," but the Marielito just shook his head. He was right to do so. In reality, Cuban Miami was in no position to hear the truth about Cuba. As Sandra Oldham said, its childhood wounds had not yet healed, and nothing, certainly no testimony of this kind, was strong enough to allow that process to begin, not as long as Fidel Castro was in power, anyway. After that, as many people in Miami would tell you, the exiles could decide what they thought, who, in some final, existential sense, they wanted to be. But in the meantime, their vision of the essential Cuban had to be that of the pre-Mariel exile, of someone who had been wrenched away and for whom the dominant issue remained that of a possible return. Whatever they heard in a classroom, or read in *The Miami Herald,* or were told by people like the Marielito I met at Miami-Dade, their will to believe remained stronger.

Their nostalgia for this Cuba of their imaginations was, of course, inseparable from their curiously unhistorical view of their own situations. For in the mind of Miami, the Cuban revolution had not been part of a historical process but an almost extrahistorical affliction. As Jorge Mas Canosa liked to say, the only thing "separating the Cubans of the island and the Cubans of the exile is one man, Fidel Castro." And to believe in that was also to believe in a kind of benign essentialism, as benign as the flora and fauna of the island so regularly conjured up for their children by an older generation of exiles, one which promised that, when Fidel Castro did finally fall, it would be possible to go back, if not actually then at least in spirit, and possible to heal the great childhood loss that so many Miami Cubans had suffered and over which, however discreetly, they continued to keen.

There was no question of letting go, for to have done so would have been akin to an act of self-mutilation. The poet and essayist Pablo Medina, who was born in Havana in 1948 and came to the United States in 1960, described this exiled state of mind well, although he was anything but critical of it, in an attractive book of memoirs he published in the late eighties called *Exiled Memories: A Cuban Childhood*. "The past was fixed in place," he wrote, describing his family's departure from Havana, "fate had conspired to cut me off from it. Suddenly I was surrounded by ice, and I jumped into the white mounds with all the enthusiasm I could muster. I renounced allegiance to the country of my birth when I became an American citizen, yet the blood still pulled and memory called. Thus it was that I became two persons, one a creature of warmth, the other the snow swimmer. The first would be forever a child dancing to the beat of the waves; the second was the adult, striving to emerge from the rivers of cold—invigorated, wise, at peace with life."

In Medina's account, there are two categories, Cubanness and Americanness, frozen and irreconcilable. Nowhere else in his book except where he talks about these questions of national character does he employ this static language or these concepts that, although they are meant benevolently, are all too reminiscent of nineteenth-century European racial fantasizing or, indeed, its modern-day Afrocentric equivalent. In the distinction between the creature of warmth that was the Cuban child and the snow swimmer that is the American adult, Medina unconsciously reproduces the black nationalist professor Leonard Jeffries's infamous categorization of the white race as "ice people" and the black race as the "people of the sun." Medina, of course, is white himself, and it is impossible to imagine from his text that he means any harm to any person or group. But his exercise of memory continually wars with his reason, just as Miami's nostalgia, however humanly understandable, often led it down paths of political fanaticism and personal self-absorption that were bound to inspire as much dread as sympathy even in the most well-disposed outsider.

Medina himself is well aware of the problem. "The truism," he writes, "that no one can ever go home again becomes a special predicament for the young exile: my childhood lies inside the bowl of distance and politics, unapproachable and thus disconnected from my adulthood. The two revolve around each other like twin stars, pulling and tugging, without hope of reconciliation. Everywhere I see Fate smiling the smile of the Sphinx." And while Medina may understand that return is impossible, his book is an argument for the preeminence of memory, the ineradicability of some Cuban essence that he discerns not only within himself but within his comrades in the exile.

"The Americanization I sought for so long," he writes in his preface to the book, "required the annihilation of memory, that tireless lady who is forever weaving and unweaving her multicolored tapestries. I don't believe anyone can do this by natural means."

Neither did many in Cuban Miami, including Raul Rodriguez —at least some of the time. It was Raul who put me on to Medina's book in the first place, pointing it out to me as we browsed in Books and Books, the fine Coral Gables bookshop whose proprietor Mitchell Kaplan makes a point of stocking and displaying the latest books on Cuba and the exile for what is his increasingly English-speaking Cuban-American clientele. As we waited for Ninon and Ruly to join us before heading out for a day on Key Biscayne, Raul picked up book after book on Havana, and interspersed his admiring comments about the beauties of the city with the remark "Ninon and I were there in 1980," or "We were all there together last August," or "We've got to get there next time we go." It was almost an afterthought for him to hand me a copy of *Exiled Memories*, but when he did so it was with the book open to the passage I have just quoted and with the remark "This is the way I feel too."

Later, he would go on to tell me that it was because he shared with Pablo Medina, whom he was at pains to point out he did not know, this sense of disconnectedness between his childhood in Havana and his adulthood in the United States that it had been so important to him to make the brief journeys he and his family had been taking back to Havana. "I can't see any other way out of our predicament here," he said. "Politics may be fine for some people, but I'm convinced that whatever happens in Cuba in the next few years will be decided by people on the island, not people here in Miami. Sure, we can help, but it's not up to us to run things. So what do *we* do? How do we confront our own losses, and all the feelings we can't resolve? Americans tell us, 'Just assimilate,' and what even the most well-intentioned among you mean . . ." His voice trailed off, as if to acknowledge the weight of the pronoun he had chosen, then he went on, "what you mean is forget about Cuba, forget about your childhoods.

"In a way, I'd like to. Certainly, when I look at Ruly I'm just as glad that he doesn't feel the same tug that I do, even though I want him to know Cuba and to love Cuba. My parents exercised the option to take me out of the country, but it was my option to reel my son back in on these trips. That doesn't mean, though, that I expect him to feel as I do. He already feels differently. And if he leaves Miami to go to school, as Ninon and I want him to do, he'll feel less, probably."

"And if he stays?" I asked.

"If he stays," Raul said, "he'll remain more of a Miami Cuban. That is the thing about Miami, those feelings die hard here. You can avoid them in Chicago, where Ninon went to college, or in New York, or California. But the thing about Miami is less that it confirms your Cubanness than that it confirms your pain. You can leave your childhood behind you when you go somewhere else, but not here. However hard people try, whether they give their kids names like Sean Perez and Jennifer Fernandez, and never speak Spanish, the disconnectedness is there. Because in Miami the past is both omnipresent and, because you can't go back—or most of us can't anyway—it's inaccessible, all at the same time."

Raul did not for a moment underestimate the price he had paid for going back to Havana three times in less than a year and a half. And he was not a rich man. Like most architectural firms in South Florida during the recession of the late eighties and early nineties, Rodriguez and Quiroga was just getting by thanks to the state and federal building projects the partners had managed to secure for themselves in the face of stiff competition. "It's insecure work," he said, "and getting more insecure every year. Even when things go well, the anxiety level is high. There are weeks when I practically live on antacids."

In the politically charged atmosphere of South Florida, where the accusation of being soft on Castro, while it might no longer make one's life physically dangerous, was certainly a professional detriment, Raul was taking a risk. Add to that the fact that while he was staunchly anti-Communist, Raul was not a Republican, like most influential South Florida Cuban-Americans (in the early nineties, President Bush's son Jeb worked for the Cuban-American builder Armando Codina, only one of the ties connecting *el exilio* with the GOP), but a Democrat, and a liberal one at that, and the risk was magnified. Besides, what made Rodriguez and Quiroga tick was Raul and his partner's presence, and to go off on these trips, and, worse, to be overwhelmed by their effect even after one had returned, was, to put it mildly, anything but good business. And yet Raul was determined to persevere.

"The cost is tremendous in every sense," he admitted. "I'm terrified before I go, and the fact that my mother, whom I adore, can't stand the thought of my going only makes things more painful for me. Then the trip itself is expensive, both in terms of what it costs to actually go and for what one spends on presents for people there. It's physically taxing—you can't believe how hot you are—never mind the psychological price. And once you return, there is terrible depression that sets in. You realize how little you can do. You love them, you love Cuba, but it's up to them. What I want to do when I return is just sleep, but of course I have to get to work. Ninon has to get back to work. Our son has to catch up with school."

Had Raul Rodriguez been temperamentally a more imprudent

man, his decision to keep returning to Cuba might have been more understandable. But he was haunted by what might happen, and, however much he might be absorbed in *el tema*, rarely lost sight of the fact that his decision might not be the right one. Nonetheless, he saw no other option. "I just feel it's worth it," he said. "The only way to bridge the gap, for me at least, is to keep returning. Ninon has mixed feelings, and, as you can imagine, Ruly doesn't really want to go at all. But they're good about it; they're sports, because they know how important it is to me to see the city, to get to know it again after all these years. You know, the part of Havana I like best is the oldest part, what they call '*la Habana intramuros,*' 'Havana within the walls.' But what I realized when we were there for the first time in 1980 is that the real wall is between the exiles and our pasts. Those are the ones I'm trying to knock down."

As much as anything, Raul was after some measure of control both over his memories and over his sense of himself as an adult. "The first time Ninon and I went to Havana, back in 1980 during the Dialogue," he said to me, "I felt as if I was again the age that I had been when we left in 1959—eleven, not thirty-two. But during that visit, I began to understand how the streets of Havana were laid out, to appreciate its beauty just as my parents must have done when they were young adults. Maybe I did not grow up during that trip, but at least I became an adolescent. And over the course of the trips we've made since, Ninon and I have grown up.

"I know it sounds crazy," he continued, "to think you can cram thirty-three years of life into four or five short visits, but that's the way it sometimes feels. Even when we returned, ten years after the first trip, with you in 1990, both Ninon and I felt so much more in control. We needed a reality check, a sense of ourselves, that we were able to contrast with our feelings of being infantilized by our situation as visitors to Cuba from the exile. Remember, we had Ruly along, and Ruly had just been born when we made the first trip in 1980. And with our son there with us, we knew we couldn't be the kids in the group, whatever we felt like inside. At least we had to behave as authority figures, as parents to our son. That made us a lot stronger. There was even a primitive level on which I could look out at Ruly, when he would stand on the balcony of our room in the Habana Libre in downtown Havana—the old Hilton; my parents used to go there all the time for dances in the old days—and realize that he was the same age in 1990 that I was in 1959, when I left. To go back with him was at the center of these trips for me. To go back with him was to change for good the sense of the past that I had had all those years in Miami. I don't say I now feel whole, but at least I have the feeling that I may be getting there.''

If, most of the time, the process of return was a way for Raul to come to grips with his exile as much as it was to come to grips with the reality of contemporary Cuba, there were other times when he was less certain that such frequent visits were a good idea. In 1990, the political possibilities had been greater. Raul did not imagine—he was anything but megalomaniacal— that his own efforts could bring about any sort of reconciliation between the Cubans of the exile and the Castro regime. But in his Catholic way, he still maintained the belief that understanding and the readiness to listen were a great part of what was required if the antipathies of thirty-one years were ever to disappear. Two years later, though, with Cuba mired in its "special period in time of peace" and the Cuban-American National Foundation helping to push a bill through the U.S. Congress that called for a tightening of the trade embargo, such a dialogue however tentative and informal, seemed all but out of the question. It was the time of the hard boys, the dominance of the "vertical" position on both sides of the Florida Strait. From a political standpoint, Raul had lost and he knew it. What was left was for him to go as a Cuban paterfamilias, and as a collector of memories.

Unsurprisingly, doubt had begun to ruin his digestion as much as any pressures at the office. "I move between two thoughts," he told me in one particularly disconsolate moment, "my work and Cuba. These days, they seem to be the only two things I'm able to think about. I had a dream the other night that I was taking an endless tour of my aunt's house in Havana—you know, Maria

Pepa, the old lady we visited. And no matter how often I tried to leave, the tour kept going on and on.

"I guess I have to change the video, don't I?" he said with a despairing smile.

The problem was, he couldn't. It was not as if Raul did not hear other voices, other arguments. His own partner, Tony Quiroga, steadfastly counseled him against going back. He was far too subtle, and too fond of Raul, to try to talk him out of it, but Quiroga made his views plain enough just the same, mostly by insisting he personally would never go back, even after Fidel Castro had fallen. "Why should I?" he'd asked me over lunch, though it was clear that his words were directed at Raul. "I am perfectly aware of what things are like in Havana today, how they have destroyed the city I loved. When the structural engineers finally do their surveys of intramural Havana, I'll bet you that half the buildings in the old town will have to be demolished. I prefer to keep my memories of what Cuba was like. If I were to return, as Raul has done, I wouldn't even have them anymore."

In part, Quiroga's ability to speak in this way stemmed from the fact that he had left Havana as an adult. Ten years older than Raul, he was already practicing architecture in Havana when the revolution came. But there was more to it than that. For every temperament a decision, and the quiet, soft-spoken Quiroga could not have been further away in his manner of address from Raul's enthusiastic, almost supercharged approach to the world. Nonetheless, they understood each other well, and cared for each other more than either was willing to say—a bond forged first as colleagues at the large Miami architectural firm of Spilis/Candela and then in the ten years in which their partnership had endured. What was nourishing for Raul, Quiroga told me, would have been poisonous for him. "For me," he continued, "to go back to Havana would be like visiting the house of people you know well, but who have moved away. You may have all sorts of connections to the place, all sorts of feelings for it and about it. But when all is said and done, you simply have no business being there anymore."

"Quiroga, the cynic," Raul said, his own affection for his

partner unmistakable. "I know you think I'm a crazy romantic—you always say so, anyhow—but I do feel whenever I go to Cuba that I belong there. Of course, I don't imagine for a second anymore, if I ever did, that I can influence the outcome, and we all know that a reconciliation between the people here and the people on the island is unlikely for now. But I am not a tourist, whatever the Cuban authorities may say. To go back is the only way I know of sorting through what I feel toward the U.S. and Cuba, the two countries to which I have a loyalty, the two flags that I love."

Under his breath, he added, "Although you know to which I have the deeper emotion."

To which Tony Quiroga, almost as quietly, replied, "Sure, Raulito, but you also know the first immigrant generation always has exactly that kind of soft spot for the country they came from, whatever the circumstances that made them leave. Ruly doesn't feel that way, does he?"

"No," Raul said.

As was often the case when he recognized even the smallest gap between his own feelings and those of his son, an expression less of sadness than of infinite tenderness crossed Raul's features. Watching him, I was reminded that pictures of Raul as a child showed him looking astonishingly like his son. It was a resemblance Raul and Ninon often commented on. Quiroga too had obviously caught the look. Before that moment he had been talking to Raul more than to me. Now, as if he sensed that his partner's case needed buttressing, he began to tell me how difficult, how alien, the whole idea of ever leaving Cuba had been for people who had grown up in Havana in the forties and fifties.

"You have to remember," he said, "that in those days nobody left, apart from a few writers and artists. It wasn't because the opportunities were not there. But in my parents' generation and even in my own, leaving meant going to the States for school or university. But after you got your degree, you came back to Havana to practice law or medicine or architecture."

"So Havana wasn't like Buenos Aires?" I asked. "It wouldn't

have been as normal for Cubans to go, say, to Madrid or New York, as Argentines always spoke of going to Paris?''

Quiroga shook his head emphatically. "It wasn't like that at all," he said. "For an Argentine to go to France was a social promotion, whereas to move from Havana to Spain? Why on earth would any of us have done that? Things were so much more prosperous, so much more advanced, in Havana in those days than they were in fascist Madrid. And there was no reason to go to the States, or, at least, we didn't think so. What I recall is a strong sense that to leave Cuba was an admission of failure. And that took on a moral dimension as well. The person who left was somehow lessened morally, rather like an Israeli nowadays who chooses not to remain in that country. Actually, I think that one of the reasons that Cubans in Miami have been so traumatized by their exile—after all, ours is not the only exile in this history of the world; we haven't suffered more than anyone else has ever suffered—is that this sanction against leaving Cuba was already present in the Cuban psyche before the revolution."

In any case, Quiroga added, "the fanatical love for all things Cuban down to the smallest folkloric detail, the type of thing that is so common here in Miami, is typical of immigrant behavior just as much as of exile behavior. It is insecure, the way that immigrant patriotism is insecure, and insistent in the way that all beleaguered people are insistent, at least if they think they can get away with it. And also, you should remember that Cubans are like all island peoples, and have an almost overdeveloped sense of their own specialness."

Quiroga waited for my response, looking across at Raul the whole time. I asked the obvious question. "Will that specialness be maintained for long in Miami?"

Raul sighed. Quiroga answered. "I suspect you already know what I think," he said. "I believe that things have gone pretty far in the opposite direction already. However much it may appear that the exile is maintaining its cohesion, many Cubans in Miami have already moved on, and more will follow. Raul doesn't agree, but I don't think we have to wait for Castro to fall for there to be a resolution to the question of whether we are really exiles or immigrants. As far as I can see, like it or not, the exile is *already* over. Don't misunderstand me. I wish with all my heart that this were not so. If Castro had not come to power, I can't imagine that I would ever have left Havana, or that most of the Cubans who live here today would have either. But Fidel did come to power, and here we are, to everyone's distress—the blacks, you Americans, ourselves—but here. And for good.''

The question though was not whether the Cubans would remain, but under what circumstances, psychic more than material, they would do so. Raul's answer was to try to go back to see what had been lost; Quiroga's was to cherish his memories, but move on. Like most Cuban Miamians, they agreed that their exile had been and continued to be a tragedy. Only the poor, I thought, as I left the offices of Rodriguez and Quiroga, those who are materially and educationally least equipped for the rigors of leaving one country for another, seem to have any hope of taking it in stride. Whatever else they may feel, they are at least not racked by the sense of having been ejected against their will from Eden. A Haitian up the road in Northeast Miami might, in the new post-assimilationist situation of the immigrant to America, reasonably think he or she has gotten the best of both worlds—patois plus employment and decent sanitation. But for people like Raul and Tony, no matter how well they might fare in their adopted country, the bitter thought would never subside that they might have been happier still back home in Havana.

A poor man may board a leaky boat in Western Haiti and think, ''Anything is better than the life I am leading.'' The proof of this is that tens of thousands have risked the passage north to Miami, even though they know their chances of getting through are small, their chances of dying at sea high. But the bourgeois leaves Havana for Miami and thinks, ''I am being torn up by my roots.'' The proof of that was everywhere to be found in Miami in 1992. Thirty-three years after the first Cuban exiles had set foot on American soil, they were thinking, ''Yes, the soil here is rich, but wasn't the red earth of Matanzas richer still? Yes, my life is fine, but wasn't my childhood sweet?''

During all the time I spent in *el exilio,* I met many people who wanted to return, and many who did not, many people who said they still cared about Cuba and many others who claimed they were happy where they were. It was easy to see that those who claimed that Cuban Miami was an ideologically uniform place, or an emotionally crude one—an allegation particularly popular among non-Cuban Miamians, who tend to take the political rhetoric of *el exilio* for its essence—were entirely mistaken. But only once did I meet a person who insisted that the exile itself had been a kind of victory, its afflictions, paradoxically, a kind of moral promotion for those who had endured them.

Teresita de Blank was a blond, slender woman of about Raul and Ninon's age. She was the daughter of an important family of Havana sugar growers and engineers, people who have arrived in Cuba from Spain at the end of the nineteenth century. To all appearances, she was someone who would have been comfortable anywhere in the world. But if she had emancipated herself to some degree from her feelings of nostalgia, she was not prepared to concede for one moment that her childhood had been any less idyllic than that of any of the other people I had met through Raul and Ninon. "People like to say now," she told me, "that the childhoods we in Havana enjoyed were the privilege of all well-off Latin Americans. But I don't agree at all. I remember in my boarding school thinking that we Cubans must be the luckiest girls in the world. The Americans were burdened with all their parents' expectations, all that Anglo-Saxon mania for success, or, do I mean, for perfection? As for the Latin Americans, my impression was that their lives were so much more closed and restricted than ours. It was as if in Havana, and I guess Cuba in general in those days, we got to have the best of both the North American and the Latin experience."

Perhaps because her own approach to the world was so insistently and, by Miami standards, so uncharacteristically realistic—"My children often come to me complaining about the unfairness of this or that, and my first response is always to remind them that life is so often unfair, so often terrible," she remarked at one point, her usually animated voice turning cool and somber for a moment—Teresita's conviction that these memories of ambrosial childhoods one heard from people who had grown up in Havana in the fifties seemed especially convincing. "My childhood was like spun sugar," she said. "It was quite literally rosy from the moment you woke up to the moment you went to sleep. On the one hand, there was very little pressure on a girl growing up in Havana society, at least before the age of thirteen. If you did not do well in school, you were likely to be told, 'Oh, don't worry, my darling, you'll marry a fine man and it won't make any difference anyway.' And besides, there were so many activities for us, so many things on offer in our beautiful, beautiful Havana that were just guaranteed to delight even the most morose child."

Even the miseries of married life in a floridly macho society like pre-Castro Cuba, Teresita remarked pensively, paradoxically could contribute to this reassuring sense that a well-born Cuban girl might entertain about her future. "If you were pretty, that was wonderful," she said, with the composed smile of someone who knows herself to be a beauty. "But even if you weren't, there was still a silver lining, because you knew in any case—you quite simply took it for granted—that your future husband would eventually take a mistress. So even these pressures were removed, since the outcome was so inevitable. And anyway, we children were completely unaware of whatever private atrocities were taking place within the family. It was the style to conceal those things then, just as today it is the style of parents to reveal everything to their kids. I don't know which is better; what I'm sure of is that we were allowed to believe that life was, well . . . wonderful. And for us, that was no fantasy."

As she tried to tease out for me the pattern of what had happened to her, Teresita was clearly under no illusions that the life she had enjoyed was one that, in retrospect anyway, she approved of. "In more ways than one," she said, "we had it too easy. You may think this is a strange thing for me to say, but while I hate Fidel Castro personally, and despise him for what he did both to my family and to my country, I, personally, am enormously grateful to him. Because I think that if I had stayed in Cuba, and lived as an adult the life that was being handed to me on a silver platter as a child, I would probably have turned into a much shallower person. Obviously, I can't speak for anybody else, but I know I am a better person for having to undergo exile, for having had to fend for myself. I had to find out who I was and what I wanted. I had to decide for myself what I believed in. And I owe this—all of it, I think—to having been forced to leave the paradise that my parents' and grandparents' generations had constructed for us in Cuba so devotedly.''

It was not that Teresita underestimated her own struggle to make a new life in the United States. She spoke knowingly of the misery of her parents' generation and the flight from reality so observable in her own. "You have to remember," she told me, "that when we first came to this country, our most profound experience was probably that of seeing at close quarters our parents' terrible frustrations. Fathers who had been immensely successful back in Cuba ended up sitting around the house—the extremely modest house, I need hardly add—sometimes literally for years on end. These self-sufficient, proud men found themselves dependent on their wives for their families' survival, and you can just imagine the effect that had on them. And, of course, among the younger generation, there were so many who became distraught at seeing their world turned upside down. All they wanted was to get married, to be taken care of, and to find a new cocoon in which to live.''

At least in the United States, however, Teresita insisted, it had been possible for Cuban exiles to follow a different trajectory—if they had the nerve, anyway. And Teresita had. Unlike many of her friends who, as she puts it, "never went to college, and never even tasted what it was like to fend for themselves," she had gone on to university, spent a long time living in New York, and, now that she and her Dutch husband had returned to Miami, endeavored not to be consumed by *el tema*. Still, though she now ran a successful business of her own, and spoke far more enthusiastically of her Bible study group than about the political controversies of the exile, Teresita had become involved in the Sugar Growers' Association, a body composed of people who had run the Cuban sugar business before the revolution. "I'm the first woman to join," she told me with a grin. "That was a shock to the others at first, but they've gotten used to me."

Her participation was largely restricted to helping draft plans for property owners to get their holdings returned to them, or, at least, to obtain compensation from a post-Castro Cuban regime. There they were, *el tema* and *el negocio,* as hard to distinguish as ever. And Teresita admitted frankly that she was motivated by a mix of "selfish and patriotic reasons." When she handed me the association's draft platform, with its preamble alluding to "the impious tyranny that has governed the Island for more than thirty years," and its ringing endnote, "God Save Cuba," she was quick to insist that unlike her colleagues, she harbored few illusions. At the sugar growers' meetings, she had learned to hold her tongue when, as she put it, political and economic realities gave way to an emotional response. She added that it wasn't that she was unemotional herself on the subject, only that "I suppose that we have become acclimated to American culture and are more realistic than our parents were. If we get to go back to Cuba, we get to go back, but I think it's counterproductive spending your time thinking about something that may never take place, or, if it does, may happen too late for you to take advantage of it."

And Teresita rejected the idea that, even were she to get some of her family's holdings returned to her, it would ever be possible to reconstitute Cuba in the way it had been for the middle and upper classes before 1959. "That life is over," she told me flatly, and it was, in retrospect, one of the most radical things one could suggest in the Miami of the exile, "and it would be better if more people here in Miami could accept the fact. It's not that I want them to stop feeling bad. I couldn't stop feeling bad myself if I tried. But I want people to remember, as I try to do, that if we Cubans had a fantastic time in the fifties, a lot of that had to do with the era. That period was wonderful in most parts of the world that were not ravaged by a war or a famine." She smiled. "Or a revolution. And my hunch is that even if Fidel Castro had not seized power, there is no way that someone growing up in Cuba in the same prosperous circumstances that I did, but ten or fifteen years later, would have enjoyed the same quality of life, or been privileged to experience the innocent world I lived in as a girl. The world has changed, and while the Cuban revolution has to be a big part of the story for us, we can't allow it to become the whole story, forever.''

5

TERESITA DE BLANK'S brave insistence that the exile, into which, by the early nineties, a fourth generation was being born in the maternity wards of Dade County, stop allowing the wounds that the Cuban revolution had inflicted upon it to dominate its dreams and actions also contained, as Teresita herself well knew, a strong element of wishful thinking. For it was one thing to talk in terms of such psychic manumission at a dinner party in Coral Gables, or, for that matter, to aspire to feel this way oneself, but quite another to find the means to put such convictions into practice. Like it or not, the entire drift of life in Miami pulled people in the opposite direction. Even Teresita herself, I realized after the initial, bracing effect of her skepticism had subsided, had not by a long shot jettisoned all the myths and assumptions of *el exilio*. When, for example, she spoke of the Cuban revolution having been for thirty-three years of exile "the whole story," or insisted that it must not be permitted to blot out everything else, she was conceding, at least implicitly, that even those Cuban-Americans most determined to get on with their new lives in the United States would continue indefinitely keeping a weather eye cast toward events on the island, continue to wait for that sweet moment when the tyrant who had blotted out their Cuban adulthoods and frozen their Cuban childhoods in the limbo of exile would himself be blotted out. In other words, while life should be normalized in the exile, it could not yet become, even for someone as lucid as Teresita, entirely normal. At least not in Miami.

The city all but exacted certain commitments from those who lived in it. It might as well have been another form of real estate tax in this conurbation of homeowners. In part, this was because to be agnostic on the question of Fidel Castro, let alone to call for a renewed dialogue or an end to the U.S. trade embargo, could be dangerous. In the sixties and seventies, people had been killed for espousing such views—for all the talk of terrorism in the United States over the previous twenty years, Miami was the only American city to experience any significant domestic terrorism, and this within its majority population—and while, by the nineties, the car bombings and the assassinations had stopped, it remained a city of bomb threats and menacing gestures. People who did not go along with the vertical position could count on being attacked on one of the Calle Ocho radio stations. Once they had been demonized, it was a foregone conclusion that they would receive a threatening phone call before the week was out. Orlando Bosch, one of the instigators of the blowing up of the Cubana de Aviación plane over Barbados in 1976, was a hero in Miami, with a citation from the City Commission to prove it. Released from a Venezuelan jail after ten years, he lived in Miami under house arrest, although this did not prevent an art gallery in Little Havana from exhibiting a collection of his prison drawings.

There were other examples, and, despite what the city's boosters liked to say, not all of them dated from a decade or two earlier. In the mid-eighties, in the most celebrated of these incidents, there had been the Cuban Museum controversy. The Cuban Museum was probably the most interesting cultural institution to have been created in the exile. Its director, Carlos Luis, was a well-known essayist and art historian, and its most prominent director, Ramon Cernuda, was not only one of the most important art collectors in Cuban Miami, but the spokesman in the exile for a number of human rights groups in Cuba, many of whose members were in Castro's jails. Their activism, however, did not blind Luis or Cernuda to the fact that there was a great deal of interesting painting going on in Cuba, and the museum organized an auction of some of this work. At the behest of some board members, however, the United States attorney for South Florida stormed into Cernuda's house, confiscating the pictures under the terms of the U.S. statute concerning "trading with the enemy." Cernuda sued, and won, but there continued to be calls for the museum to be ousted from its city-owned premises long after the original controversy faded.

The tendency in Miami to talk about such events as if they were ancient history was not borne out by the realities on the ground. The proposed boycott of *The Miami Herald* by some members of the Cuban-American National Foundation—a boycott which, though he did not explicitly endorse, Mayor Xavier Suarez was on record as viewing with understanding—was not ancient history, nor were the attacks on Francisco Aruca, whom Jorge Mas Canosa had described as Castro's radio announcer in Miami. In the summer of 1992, the Cuban Museum announced plans to exhibit the work of Tomas Sanchez, a well-known painter still living in Cuba, and already the airwaves in Miami were heating up. That was the same summer that Americas Watch, a human rights organization more usually found investigating Salvadoran death squads or, for that matter, the treatment of political prisoners in Cuba, issued a report on freedom of expression in Miami with the glum and accurate title "Dangerous Dialogue."

But the tendency of non-Cuban liberals in Miami, and many informed outsiders, to see only the city of right-wing exiles hell-bent on imposing their views on what was, from a political point of view, an extremely heterodox community was itself extremely reductive. Incidents like the Cuban Museum controversy had not taken place in either a historical or an emotional vacuum, and to speak as if they did, or to content oneself with observing that right-wing Cubans in Miami seemed to have the same totalitarian tendencies as those they claimed to abhor in Fidel Castro, was to miss the point of what was really going on. For Miami did not simply exact certain views, it also freely engendered them. People who had little sympathy with the Foundation, and none whatsoever with Orlando Bosch or the radio jockeys of Calle Ocho, often unwillingly found themselves sharing certain emotional presuppositions with them.

Even Raul Rodriguez, who could not have been more contemptuous of the Foundation's bullying style, occasionally was forced to explain to non-Cuban Miamians why the Foundation's approach resonated with so many Cuban-Americans. In the wake of Mas Canosa's attacks on *The Miami Herald,* Raul, who was then president of the community organization Facts About Cuban Exiles, FACE, was invited by David Lawrence, Jr., the paper's publisher, to come to a meeting of the editorial board. Raul had made it clear already that he was completely opposed to a boycott, and, if he were forced to choose, would support the *Herald.* Nonetheless, when he led the delegation from FACE into the publisher's conference room, Raul began by trying to explain to his non-Cuban interlocutors what lay behind the rhetoric, and why, when Mas Canosa bought space on Miami city buses to display signs reading, "I don't believe *The Miami Herald,*" so many Miami Cubans felt at least a momentary flash of agreement.

"The first thing you have to understand," Raul told the board, "is how much pain there is in this community. I don't mean in terms of being a Cuban in Miami. From that point of view things are much better these days. After all, most people here think that when the Berlin Wall came down in 1989, Cuban Miami won the war. If you think back, you can see the point. Imagine what it was like to be a Cuban-American in the nineteen-sixties when the whole United States seemed to be veering to the left, and this community was almost as disdained in political and cultural circles in New York as it was by the Communists in Havana. *That* was difficult. What is going on now is not, at least by comparison.

"But, as I started out by saying, there is still so much pain in this community, such a sense of loss and of hurt, that it really shouldn't surprise you when people overreact. Mas Canosa only represents one segment of Cuban Miami, but what he has done very ably is to capitalize on the community's pain. You will hear lots of opinions expressed by the people in this room, but I don't think anyone here would deny that we are all prey to these feelings you see in an extreme form in the boycott talk. And until Castro falls, and we have the opportunity to decide whether or not we want to return to Cuba, I don't think they are likely to go away."

The controversy made little sense otherwise. Viewed from a distance, it was actually hard to tell why the Cuban-American National Foundation had become so upset with *The Miami Herald* in the first place. After all, there had been other influential American ethnic groups in other American cities who regularly complained about the treatment their communities had received, or about the stances their local papers had taken on politics in the old country, without the disputes turning into affairs of boycott and intimidation. There were American Jewish groups, particularly during the high-water period of right-wing governments in Israel, who had been incensed at the treatment of the Jewish state by papers like *The Boston Globe* and *The Washington Post*. And while it was true that the peculiar stridency of the Foundation would have been hard to match in any other community, it was also true that Mas Canosa and his followers had struck a responsive chord in Cuban Miami. That was the salient difference.

For there were many in the exile who did believe that the *Herald* was biased against the Cuban community. In part, this referred back to the period before the late seventies when few Cuban-Americans worked for the *Herald* and the paper tended to treat Cuban Miami as if it were some insignificant ethnic enclave, a Chinatown writ slightly larger than such ethnic enclaves usually are. Not only were few events taking place within Cuban Miami covered during this period, but the management team then running the paper had attempted to transform its circulation base from Dade County, which was becoming increasingly Cuban, to suburban Broward County, to which many non-Cuban Miamians were now moving. That effort had failed, however, and, realizing that either the *Herald* made a go of things in Miami or it went out of business, the paper's parent company, Knight-Ridder, installed a new management team, led by the Spanish-speaking Lawrence, beefed up *El Nuevo Herald,* and went from an attitude that relegated news of the Cuban community to the back pages to one that prominently featured it.

A similar transformation took place in the *Herald*'s coverage of Cuba itself. There had been a time when Mas Canosa's claim that the paper was turning a blind eye to Castro's crimes against Cubans on the island would have been hard to dispute. By and large, the paper's editorial stance was the same as that of other liberal American newspapers and gave the tyrant—this was putting the matter charitably—the benefit of the doubt. What stories that did appear about political prisoners were far outweighed, in terms of space and where they were featured, by details of Cuban advances in health care and education. Indeed, the *Herald* was so obdurately silent that, in a famous incident in the seventies, a group composed mainly of young, former Cuban political prisoners chained themselves to the paper's front doors to protest the absence of coverage of political repression on the island, which, in many cases, concerned the relatives not only of the demonstrators themselves, but of more than a few readers of *The Miami Herald* in Dade County.

But things had changed enormously since that time. Ramon Mestre, who had led the demonstration, and whose father had spent seventeen years in a Cuban prison, was now a member of the *Herald*'s editorial board. And a visitor to Miami in the early nineties would have been hard-pressed to avoid the impression that at the *Herald* international news basically meant Latin American news, and that Latin American news basically meant Cuba first, with every other country trailing behind. Disgruntled reporters on the paper even reported shouting matches in the newsroom between journalists eager to get some space for their reports on other parts of the world and senior management who insisted that pride of place be given to Cuba first, and, in a nod toward Jewish Miami Beach, Israel second. According to one such account, a senior, non-Cuban official at the paper was talking on and on to some editors about the need to increase coverage of Cuba when, in exasperation, a Cuban-American journalist interrupted to say that, for her part, she was interested in other things besides the Caribbean, whatever her ethnic background might be.

In their less inflamed moments, even members of the Cuban-American National Foundation all but conceded the point. Rene Silva, an area coordinator for the organization in South Florida, wrote in a special edition of the CANF's broadsheet, *Fundación*, that one of the things that made living in Miami special for a Cuban exile was that while anywhere else in the United States, news reports about Cuba were "skimpy," and required one to engage in *un esfuerzo investigadorio,*" "an investigative effort," in Miami such information was readily available. And certainly anyone trying to follow Cuban as well as, obviously, Cuban exile affairs in the American daily press would have been lost without the *Herald*.

But not only did the slights of the past still rankle in Cuban Miami, and not just among the stalwarts of the Foundation, but other, more recent grievances had come to the fore as well. For Jorge Mas Canosa, the *Herald*'s coverage might well have become more copious, but it had not yet become more balanced. Mas Canosa complained that the *Herald*'s reporters paid attention to dissidents who were opposed to the Foundation, not to those who supported its goals—particularly the tightening of the embargo—despite the fact that, at least according to Andres Oppenheimer, the *Herald*'s Argentine-born chief Latin American correspondent, who had covered Cuba extensively, very few such people could actually be found on the island. Still, Mas Canosa persevered, and by the time he began to organize the boycott campaign, Knight-Ridder was running scared. One reporter at the *Herald* groused to me privately that "if David Lawrence had only told Mas to fuck off when all this began, none of this would have happened. Instead, we backpedaled and backpedaled. We allowed Jorge Mas to refuse to talk to any reporter he didn't care for, instead of saying, 'Mr. Mas, talk to everyone or no one.' And worst of all, we started featuring dissidents in Cuba whose views coincided with those of the Foundation, even though we knew perfectly well that these people were a tiny fringe within the dissident movement itself, and that the important human rights leaders on the island, from Gustavo Arcos to Elizardo Sánchez, and from Maria Cruz Varela to Vladimir Roca, all wanted exactly what the Foundation was campaigning so hard against—a dialogue between the U.S. and Cuban governments, and between the exile and the Cuban authorities as well.''

This was certainly true as far as it went. The spectacle of the *Herald*'s temporizing had caused a great deal of indignation, both among liberal Cuban-Americans and, though not necessarily for the right reasons, among non-Cuban Miamians for whom the controversy only confirmed their worst stereotypes of the exile. At the height of the controversy, I was driving in Coral Gables with a friend from Miami Beach when, at a stoplight, one of the city buses bearing the poster saying "I don't believe *The Miami Herald*" pulled up alongside us. My friend stared at it for a long moment, and then, with a shake of his head, said grimly, "Well, I don't believe Cuban Miamians either. What that sign really says is 'I don't give a damn about freedom of the press. I don't have to; I'm Cuban.' " It was neither the first nor the last time I heard such a sentiment.

And yet it, too, did nothing to explain why otherwise sensible people in Cuban Miami resonated to Mas Canosa's attacks. Many of them, after all, were by no means convinced that Mas Canosa, who was rumored to view himself as in line for the presidency of Cuba after Castro's fall, was to be trusted politically, or, for that matter, that those on the island who agreed with him were particularly to be trusted either. But when Mas Canosa's attacks on the *Herald* came up in casual conversation, many Cuban Miamians I met, when pressed, would say the same thing: "At least Mas Canosa is doing something." And by this they meant not so much keeping the *Herald* honest, or, for that matter trying to get it to mend its ways—although that certainly had its attractions for many—as keeping the cause of Cuba, *la causa sagrada,* "the sacred cause," alive. This was a goal that united, it seemed, right-wing activists in Hialeah, young Cuban professionals from Coral Gables (yuccas, they were called, for "young, up-and-coming Cuban-Americans"), retirees in Kendall, and, for that matter, the purportedly liberal mayor of Miami, the Honorable Xavier L. Suarez.

Suarez was a complicated figure. Despite his sympathy for those who had wanted to close down the Cuban Museum, he had presented himself, from his first successful campaign in 1985, as an ecumenical figure, someone who was not going to be bound by the parochial concerns of *el exilio,* as other Cuban-American officeholders had been. He certainly had the credentials, having been educated at a Catholic university in Pennsylvania and at Harvard's Kennedy School of Government. And, during his two terms as mayor, he had successfully cobbled together a coalition that transcended ethnic and party lines (Suarez had run as an independent) and put in place an administration to which no hint of venality or scandal had attached itself—a rarity in Miami political history. Suarez also made a great point of expressing his concern for poor people and non-Cuban immigrants to South Florida. In 1992, when the U.S. Coast Guard was forcibly turning back Haitian boat people in the Florida Strait, Suarez had a bumper sticker put on his official car that read, "Deter Drugs, Not Haitians."

In 1992, it was generally understood in Miami that Suarez would face a serious challenge from Miriam Alonso, a far more right-wing Cuban-American city commissioner who had long been a vocal critic of his policies. Perhaps in siding with those attacking the *Herald,* Suarez was doing no more than shoring up his base in Cuban Miami. Nonetheless, most people who knew him were surprised when he sided with the paper's critics. And his support consisted in far more than the issuing of a press release or two. At the height of the imbroglio between Mas Canosa and the *Herald,* the Foundation began to promote another organization, the Cuban-American Anti-Defamation League, whose business it was to be to combat slanders in the press against the Cuban community. Jorge Mas and several other Foundation board members joined immediately, and so, enthusiastically, did Xavier Suarez. When he was asked whether he saw anything inappropriate about the sitting mayor of Miami joining a group that seemed dedicated to bringing the city's leading newspaper into line, Suarez was emphatic. "I've accepted all the institutions of this country," he told a meeting of FACE, "but I find the negative press an institution very much in need of reform." Then he added, "When I complain about the treatment the *Herald* gives the Cuban community perhaps it really is a cultural difference."

In an America that was becoming both balkanized and global-
ized at once, a country in which African-Americans were invent-
ing their own "Africatude," but in which, simultaneously, pacts
like the North American Free Trade Agreement were diluting
notions of national borders and fixed identities—whether of people or of consumer goods—a phrase like "cultural difference,"
by which Suarez simply meant that Cubans saw things in a particularly "Cuban" way, was little more than a piece of the multicultural background noise of the era. Obviously, Suarez did not
mean that, say, cannibalism was a cultural difference that should
have been respected, or clitoridectomy, or suttee, although the
logic of his position probably led him closer to such a stance than
he knew. What he did mean, however, what came through at that
FACE meeting in a private dining room in the Grand Bay Hotel
in Coconut Grove with passionate sincerity, was that he felt
affronted, and, in this, it was hard not to feel that most of the
Cubans in the room, and, for that matter, in Greater Miami as
well, at least partly agreed with him.

It was not a question of specifics. Suarez's own view of what
kind of newspaper he might have wished *The Miami Herald* to be
was hazy. But he was in no doubt, it seemed, as to what kind of
newspaper he did not consider acceptable. He had arrived at the
FACE lunch late, in a swirl of bodyguards, aides, and apologies
in two languages. Before sitting down, he had handed out to the
FACE board members Xeroxed copies of an article he had prepared on the obligations of the press toward the community, by
which, it turned out, he meant the Cuban community, the exile.
The article was extraordinary, fierce, intransigent, and patheti-
cally naive all at the same time. It began with a bit of throat-
clearing about the noble ideals of the First Amendment to the
United States Constitution, but it soon got down to business.
"No discussion," Suarez had written, "of the relationship between the media and an exile group can shed much light without
an understanding of the way the media uses this constitutional
right in order to shield themselves from criticism when they
misstate fact, slant news and opinion, omit important aspects of
a matter while giving prominence to the trivial, and tarnish un-

duly the individual and collective good name of an ethnic group.''

If he was to be taken at his word, both at that meeting and, later, when I spoke to him about his arguments, Suarez's ambition was nothing less than the wholesale reform of the American press. Certainly, his view of rights under American law was novel. He asserted, for example, that the ''right'' to have one's name respected was as important as freedom of the press, even though it had not been viewed as such by the framers of the American Constitution. Moreover, it was hard to know whether Suarez meant his strictures to apply to everyone. For example, did everyone have the right to have his or her name respected, or were there to be exceptions? Was the *Herald* obliged to hew to this approach, but the Calle Ocho radio stations, where calumny was almost always the main course, were not? Xavier Suarez did not say. Instead, he charged ahead. ''The law of defamation,'' he wrote, ''has a glaring deficiency: It does not permit a lawsuit for libel to be filed by a larger aggrieved party, such as an entire ethnic or national-origin group. Cubans as a whole, or even Cuban-Americans, cannot file suit when a newspaper ridicules our image. When that happens, it is incumbent to explore other avenues of redress, including the simple but compelling tactic of a public critique (a condemnation) of the medium committing the transgression.''

There were many curiosities about the language of Suarez's essay. It oscillated between the vernacular of lawyers, of civic proclamations, of contracts, and of the moral philosophy Suarez had doubtless picked up from his Augustinian professors at Villanova University near Philadelphia. To speak of ''slanted'' opinion was surely something of a contradiction in terms. What else was opinion supposed to be? And for the mayor of Miami to accuse *The Miami Herald* of giving prominence to the trivial, when in a tourist-dependent economy like Miami's an emphasis on the ephemeral was, to put it charitably, part of the boosterist game plan, was surely a little overdone. It was not as if Suarez were complaining that Miami, in its more self-aggrandizing moments, liked to present itself either as ''the Magic City'' or, in attempting to lure investors, as ''the capital of Latin America,'' two misrepresentations of the first order, since no big city is magical these days—Miami being, among other things, the auto theft capital of America, according to 1992 FBI statistics—and if the capital of Latin America was anywhere, it was in Caracas, or Mexico City, or Buenos Aires, not in South Florida. But those misrepresentations were all right, it appeared, since they were exaggerations that went with *el negocio,* with business, while Suarez, of course, was really talking about *el tema.*

Other rhetorical tropes were less surprising. When Suarez wrote in such a way as to elide the distinction between Cubans and Cuban-Americans, he was simply recapitulating the normal Miami line that, as Mas Canosa was always saying, there was only one Cuban people, ten percent of whom lived in Miami and the rest in Cuba itself. And when Suarez alluded to the press's "transgressions," the language of his Catholic training had clearly fused with the religious rhetoric of classical Cuban nationalism, an idiom in which José Martí, the animating spirit of Cuban independence in the nineteenth century, was as often called *el Apóstol,* "the Apostle"—as if he had been St. Paul—as he was mentioned by name. Cuba, after all, was not "the cause" but "the *sacred* cause," and it stood to reason that those who would do anything that could be perceived as against its interests would not be viewed simply as people who disagreed, or took an agnostic view, but as heretics, enemies of the faith, transgressors.

This would have been obvious to anyone reading Suarez's essay. But the most curious, and, as it happened, ominous, linguistic stratagem he employed would have been apparent only to someone who knew Spanish and was familiar with Cuban political life, not simply in Miami but on the island as well. For when he spoke of a "public critique," Suarez, perhaps feeling he had not made himself sufficiently clear, had felt it necessary to add, in parentheses, the words "a condemnation." In English, the term is amorphous, and could suggest almost anything, from a judicial punishment to a stiff letter to the editor. But translate it back into Spanish, and a far more specific reference emerged. In the Cuban context, the first thing that came to mind was *un acto*

de repudio, "an act of repudiation." The demonstrations down
Fifth Avenue in Miramar in 1980, denouncing those who wanted
to flee at Mariel, had been *actos de repudio.* The women who,
whether instigated by the authorities or on their own account, had
barged into the Havana apartment of the dissident poet Maria
Cruz Varela, stuffed the leaflets she had been distributing clan-
destinely into her mouth, forced her to swallow a few, and then
kicked her down the stairs were committing—in Miami, one had
seen the tape in which they used the words, picked up from
Cuban state television—an *acto de repudio.*

And the custom had spread to Miami. When demonstrators had
clustered outside Francisco Aruca's radio station, they told reporters they were there as an act of repudiation. When veterans of
Brigade 2506 attacked Rafael Penalver, a prominent local attorney, whose work on behalf of those refugees from Mariel still
detained by the American authorities on the grounds of their
criminal records in Cuba had made him a hero to many in Cuban
Miami, this too was presented as an *acto de repudio.* Indeed,
Aruca told me later, with some amusement, that when he had met
Elizardo Sánchez in Havana (Aruca, though he tilted toward the
regime, skillfully kept his channels open toward its opponents),
during the brief period when that heroic man had been allowed
out of jail by the Cuban authorities, Sánchez's first words to him
had been, "Well, *chico,* I guess we've both managed to survive
our respective *actos de repudio.*" And yet it was this baleful
tactic that Xavier Suarez believed needed to be employed as a
counterbalance to the errors and slanted reporting of *The Miami
Herald.*

Anyone listening to Xavier Suarez that day would have testified that, whatever political advantage he hoped to draw from this
vertical position, he was a man who believed himself to be speaking the truth. And yet it was hard to see quite why he felt so
indignant. Mas Canosa, whatever one thought of him, had to care
about how the *Herald* reported on "his" dissidents, as opposed
to those aligned with his exile opponents in la Plataforma. And
whether or not Mas Canosa's own plans for a political career in
a post-Castro Cuba were likely to bear fruit, that he would have

such a career, if he lived and Castro fell, was undeniable. But Suarez was different. He wasn't going to become mayor of Santiago de Cuba or Havana, nor, unlike Mas Canosa, had he come to manhood in the fevered milieu of exile politics. He was Cuban-American, and had made his career based on that fact. But, if anything, Suarez's feelings seemed as strong as if not stronger than Mas Canosa's, and that they did testified as eloquently to the living quality of the exile's pain as Suarez's mixed metaphors and bizarre linguistic flourishes testified to his underlying intellectual confusions.

The point was not any particular controversy—a difference of opinion about Cuban dissident politics, say, or the resentment of Suarez and his friends at seeing the *Herald* report on the financial difficulties of some important local banker. Suarez might well attribute the *Herald*'s readiness to believe a particular allegation about a Cuban to some long-standing anti-Cuban animus at the paper—and it was even possible that in at least an instance or two he might have been right—but the feeling underlying his rage had far more to do with the situation of *el exilio,* the exile of the assimilated, Americanized Suarez as much as of Mas Canosa or any other exile politico, than it did with any particular event or controversy. It was indignation born out of Cuban Miami's sense of beleaguerment, and, viewed from this perspective, what was most important about the attacks on the *Herald* was not the ostensible causes, but their subtext. It was as if much of Cuban Miami, across most of its political spectrum (which was wider than most outsiders believed), had been saying to the larger South Florida community, "Look at us, we're hurting. Here we are trying to keep our memories alive and our belief in Cuba and in ourselves strong. Then the *Herald* comes along, and, in its refusal to support us in this effort, in its willingness to undermine us for nothing more consequential than something that makes a good story, saps us of our strength and of our belief. Is that right? Is that fair? Is that neighborly?"

In the closing section of his essay, Suarez all but said as much. It is the cry from the heart of the immigrant who has been materially successful, but is emotionally still on life support. The media in the United States, Suarez wrote, "cannot easily comprehend the consternation caused in the minds and hearts of immigrants when they find that the media here care not one whit if the coverage tends to promote good will, ennoble the values of society, enhance understanding among various groups. They are puzzled when the media seeks out controversy, spends innumerable resources to uncover personal transgressions by prominent members of society, [rather than giving] more prominence to an enterprise's first million dollars in profit.''

To the frustration of the immigrant, who cannot, or at least affects not to be able to, fathom why a newspaper is more interested in scandals than in testimonials, *el exilio* could add the claim that it, in historical particular, stood in need of good news, both about its present and about its future, about Cuba and about the United States. Suarez in his essay quoted approvingly the distinction Al Neuharth, the publisher of *USA Today*, had made between the "journalism of hope" he wanted his own pages to reflect and the "journalism of despair" that he saw as permeating the pages of newspapers like *The Washington Post, The New York Times*, and, of course, *The Miami Herald*. For the exile, Suarez insisted, such an approach was essential. "An exile community," he wrote, "can survive only with strong doses of hope. The cynicism of the media, the despair that it breeds compounds the hopelessness of an exile which is now in its fourth decade.'' The Cuban-American Anti-Defamation League, Suarez concluded, wanted to combat the American press's "Manichaean view of man.'' It hoped to inject "not only its news perspectives but its mood of hope and triumph over the evil of tyranny.''

In their conclusion, Suarez's words were pure campaign rhetoric, and, as everyone at the FACE luncheon that day understood perfectly well, bashing the *Herald* was certainly going to win Xavier Suarez more votes in Miami than it lost him. That same week, a New Jersey congressman who had written a bill calling for the tightening of the U.S. trade embargo against Cuba—the Cuban Democracy Act, he called it—had addressed a Foundation-sponsored rally in Miami and begun with the words, "I'm Bob Torricelli, the man *The Miami Herald* loves to hate.''

A year later, this same Congressman Torricelli was identified as being the fifth most successful fund-raiser in the House of Representatives. And if the Italian-American Torricelli could succeed using this kind of language, it behooved the homegrown Suarez to do no less. His arguments might not hold up under scrutiny, but that was not the point. When, for example, he wrote that American reporters should recognize their own "arrogant lack of awareness . . . that their strange system of publishing is not the only one around [and] seem blissfully ignorant of the journalistic culture of other nations, including the predominant one in this hemisphere," Suarez was not calling for a return to the kind of newspapers that existed in Cuba before the revolution and reflected absolutely the view of one political party or proprietor—in postrevolutionary Cuba, another example came to mind as well: *Granma*—so much as he was asking that the press try to understand.

For on its deepest, and its only respectable, level, Suarez's essay was another Miami Cuban cry from the heart, another manifestation of the unhealed wound that exile represented even for a successful politician like Xavier Suarez, or, for that matter, the group of successful entrepreneurs, bankers, businesswomen, and civic leaders who had assembled for the FACE luncheon that afternoon in Coconut Grove. Those people had their differences with Suarez, and several did not plan to back him in his next bid for the mayoralty. But by and large, most seemed to share his intuition that, in its refusal to help the exile cause, the *Herald* might actually be harming it. And, on reflection, such feelings were probably only to be expected. Not for nothing had a phrase coined in the sixties by a now nearly forgotten American radical named Eldridge Cleaver acquired such renown. "If you're not part of the solution, baby," Cleaver had said, "you're part of the problem." And if this statement was as demonstrably false in 1992 as it had been in 1967, that did not make it less attractive to any group that felt itself to be under siege, whether that group was Cleaver's own Black Panther party or, across the yawning gap of time, race, and political inclination, the Cuban exiles of Dade County, Florida.

But *el exilio* could endure only if it could maintain its faith. That was the crux of the matter. It was as if, in every story in *The Miami Herald* that might possibly be construed as unfriendly, many Miami Cubans had discerned the imputation that their faith was an illusion, that their hopes were vain. The fact that it was not the job of a newspaper, whether in Bogotá or in Miami, to provide such hope—whatever Xavier Suarez might have claimed—and that, indeed, if anything the *Herald*'s coverage of the exile was probably not critical enough, was beside the point, just as the specific stories about which the new Cuban Civil Rights Committee was up in arms were beside the point. Any dose of realism would have been unwelcome, because any dose of realism would have threatened to impeach these sustaining Cuban dreams. "You know how the Jews say, 'Next year in Jerusalem'?" one of the FACE board members asked me, after Suarez had left. "Well, we Cubans have always said, 'Next year in Havana.' You've probably heard that. But I bet you don't know that just like the Jews, what is important to us is that we say it, that we keep on saying it. That's what unites us, that feeling. It's an emotional thing, something no one should try to take away."

What she was saying was clear. The *Herald* had tried, as many people and forces in Miami in 1992 were trying, to destroy the exile's hope and its pride. There was Fidel Castro's endurance, against all odds, three years after the Berlin Wall had fallen. That had been a bitter blow, one that the exile had not yet fully assimilated. Meanwhile, in Miami, the portents of the end of the exile, with or without the collapse of Communism on the island, were clear and getting clearer. There was the gradual assimilation of the children of Miami, a phenomenon that most people acknowledged, and, in any case, since so many could be found speaking Spanish to each other and English to their kids, they were scarcely in a position to deny. And there was increasing intermarriage between Cubans and non-Cubans, something that was less easily discussed, but almost as ubiquitous. Beyond that, there were the rigors of professional life. One could not, when all was said and done, be a professional Cuban all the time; one had to be a professional doctor, or lawyer, or businessman, and in an increasingly unleisured, parlous economy the professional stakes only grew higher every year. In 1990, Raul Rodriguez had worried about the effect his family's visit to Cuba would have on his reputation. In 1991, planning another visit, he mostly worried whether he could afford to be away from the office for that much time.

Under the circumstances, the community's anger and its pain could only be directed outward. Cuban-Americans were not, after thirty-three years of economic struggle in the United States, about to repudiate their own work ethic, particularly now when times were difficult. Nor were most of them likely to blame Washington, understanding as they did that because the Cuban-American lobby in the capital had been enormously successful, miraculously so in light of the fact that the richest Cuban exile families, the Fanjuls, the Bacardis, and the rest, had shown themselves largely indifferent to the cause, such a course would be truly dangerous. And people in Cuban Miami were hardly likely, devoted to their families to the point of obsession as they generally were, to reproach their own offspring for becoming Americanized or disown them for falling in love and marrying non-Cubans. That left only a few targets, of course, besides Fidel Castro himself, and a few homegrown Antichrists like Francisco Aruca, but just as much unhappiness and confusion. Which was why *The Miami Herald,* with its past of ignoring Cuban Miami, and its present of being skeptical about its fondest hopes, seemed so culpable, even to those who were otherwise far from likely to be drawn to the idea of a boycott, let alone an act of repudiation.

What was at stake, in the end, was the significance of Miami itself. What the *Herald* controversy finally revealed was not a coincidence of exile opinion—that really was the view from the outside—but a coincidence of feeling. The point about the newspaper was not that it was the *Herald* but *The MIAMI Herald,* the recorder of the exile itself, a recorder, in the view of most Cuban Miamians, that had fallen down on the job. It did no good to say that the paper had been going about its business long before Miami became a Cuban city. In the view of the exile, everything had changed since then for them and their hometown newspaper should have reflected that. Didn't the people at the *Herald* understand that Miami was different? When Rene Silva, for example, spoke of his experience of living for twenty years "on the outside," there would have been few Cuban Miamians who would not quickly have understood that he was referring not to the decades he had spent in exile from Cuba but to the years he had spent as a Cuban away from Miami. This was the community the *Herald* now served; why couldn't it simply acknowledge the fact that Miami was, as Silva put it, "the capital of the exile"?

And in this capital people were hurting. Silva himself had referred to his love of Cuba as a "sacred illness." That was an extreme, politicized position. And yet the image of the exile's feeling for Cuba as being something that was quite beyond people's reason, quite beyond their control, was something that one heard all the time in Cuban Miami. Its most common formulation was a simple "I feel Cuban"; its underlying theme that until Castro fell, everything had to remain in place. Such emotions could even produce a certain tolerance where none might otherwise have existed. At cocktail parties in Miami that I attended with Raul and Ninon Rodriguez, I was often buttonholed by acquaintances of Raul's who, while shaking their heads at the frequency or even the folly of his visits to Havana, would often use the same exculpatory formulation of illness or obsession to account for them. "Raul's not pro-Castro," one elderly stalwart of the Foundation sputtered, admonishing his nephew who had referred sneeringly to Raul's most recent trip. "He's just on a mission from God. How could he resist returning to our beautiful country?"

Had the thought occurred to him, this man might have found that the phrase "sacred illness" applied just as well, not simply to Raul, but to the exile as a whole. The fury toward the *Herald* was, in this sense, less evidence of Cuban intolerance, or political immaturity, or self-absorption, than a symptom. And whether it was Xavier Suarez going out on an irrational limb, and, like a kind of totalitarian Don Quixote, claiming the right to single-handedly reform the American press, or Teresita de Blank helping her father's old friends in the Sugar Growers' Association draft their claims for restitution of property they had lost more than three decades before, or Ramon Cernuda bravely exhibiting paintings from Cuba, or Raul Rodriguez, with his oft-declared intention of making those regular visits to Havana that were so controversial in Miami and simultaneously so painful and so uplifting for him, many people in Cuban Miami seemed absorbed in treating their sacred illnesses with whatever palliatives they could find.

6

It was a paradox, but by the fall of 1992, not only was *el exilio*'s sacred illness growing worse—the prospect of return made that predictable—but its painful frustration was getting worse as well. This should not have been surprising. The prognosis for Cuba's transformation, and, more critically, the timetable for it, had, it was clear, been far too optimistic. And yet this was not Cuban Miami's doing. This time, instead of attempting, as it had done so often in the past, to sway public opinion in the rest of the world, the exile itself had been swayed by all the triumphalist talk that was emanating from Washington and the American punditocracy. All this talk that, in the words of a fine book published that year by the *Herald*'s Andres Oppenheimer on the situation in contemporary Cuba, it really was "Castro's final hour," and, more generally, the insistence that Communism had been permanently relegated to the dustbin of history—assuming there would be any more history, that is; according to Francis Fukuyama, a leading conservative policy intellectual, that category too had reached its end—had put an end to the deep-seated resignation of some and the ability to be patient of others. Hope, as Xavier Suarez had said, might be needed to keep the community's morale intact, but too much hope coming too suddenly, and, after that, the need to defer this hope yet again, was just as likely to demoralize.

For Cuban Miamians to have talked of Fidel Castro as an antediluvian totalitarian, and of the Cuba he had refashioned as a society that could not endure, had been one thing. To hear people in New York and Washington, Madrid and Mexico City, suddenly saying the same thing was another. Had Castro fallen, of course, then Miami's ideological vindication would have seemed sweet. But collapse of the Soviet Union or no collapse of the Soviet Union, the dictator remained in power, and that made even vindication hard to bear. So Cuban Miami, as it had done so often in the past thirty-three years, began to get angry again, if only as a way of medicating its keen disappointment over the doomed tyrant's obstinate refusal to heed history's marching orders and just . . . fall. There was more blame for Aruca—Castro's voice in Miami, as a member of the Cuban-American National Foundation called him at a congressional hearing on the Cuban Democracy Act. There was blame for the Americas Watch report "Dangerous Dialogue," and the imputation that this document was somehow helping Castro stay in control. "We know exactly why this has been produced now," Luis Figueroa, a leader of a coalition called Unidad Cubana, "Cuban Unity," told a news conference in Miami. "This report appears precisely at the most critical moment for Fidel Castro," he continued, insisting that it was meant to "prevent Cuban exiles from continuing to enjoy credibility and respect in American public opinion." And, once again, there was blame for *The Miami Herald.*

The irony was that, as even the Castro government's defenders were being forced to admit, the news from Cuba was increasingly dire. Both sympathizers with the regime returning to New York or San Francisco and Cuban-Americans returning to Miami after their family visits to the island told much the same stories. Even the regime's vaunted health care system, the trump card that most revolutionary loyalists would play when taxed with its human rights abuses and other felonies like the forcible sequestration of anyone testing seropositive for HIV, was being hollowed out by scarcity. A doctor on call in every neighborhood was not, in the end, tremendously useful if the medicines that he or she prescribed were unavailable. Meanwhile, Castro's own pronouncements suggested that he was becoming more and more of an old-fashioned Latin American *caudillo* of the most florid and familiar type. Even the Maximum Leader's admirers outside Cuba were conceding something was amiss. They could hardly have done otherwise, for the examples of his erratic behavior were proliferating. The man who had spent a billion dollars of the Cuban treasury's hard currency reserves on developing the drug interferon, which he erroneously believed to be a cure for cancer, who had imported tons of topsoil from the Hungarian wine country in an unsuccessful effort to create a Cuban viniculture, and who had decreed that the Hereford cattle herds of Cuba be cross-bred with Indian zebu strains in the vain hope of increasing dairy yields now deemed himself to be an ace meteorologist. In the wake of the devastating flood that struck Havana in the summer of 1991, Castro upbraided *Granma* for failing to publish the warnings he had given to the newspaper's editors that the disturbances were about to take place.

All of this promiscuous pontificating on matters great and small was eerily reminiscent not simply of other historic Communist tyrant-loons, from Stalin, who had ordered a dozen books on linguistics ghostwritten for him, to North Korea's Kim Il Sung, who had tried to establish a similarly exalted place for himself as a moral philosopher, but of one of Colonel Aureliano Buendía's crazier monologues in Castro's friend Gabriel García Márquez's novel *One Hundred Years of Solitude*. "Sometimes," a friend of the great Colombian novelist once remarked to me waspishly, when the subject of García Márquez's continuing loyalty to the Cuban revolution was broached at a dinner party in Mexico City, "I think the secret reason Gabo remains such a strong supporter of Fidel is not that he still sympathizes wholeheartedly with the revolution—he used to, of course, but now who can say?—but that *as a writer* he can't stand the idea of losing access to a man who is slowly but surely turning into one of his own characters. Just to be able to witness such a process must be irresistible, and has to count a great deal more than any ideological considerations for an artist of his caliber."

Still, whatever the appeals of the chance of watching this "magical Communism" unfold, by 1991 even García Márquez was spending less time in Havana than he had for twenty years.

The house that he had been given by a grateful regime—and with good reason; the services of García Márquez to the Cuban revolution, which he had defended ardently and with panache all over the world for three decades—lay empty for most of the year, although it is unlikely that this was any consolation to its original owners, the bourgeois Miramar family that had long before resettled in Coral Gables, Florida. That said, if García Márquez continued to keep his doubts about the revolution to himself, eschewing all public acknowledgment of whatever second thoughts he might now harbor, they were becoming easier to detect in his art. The novel he published in 1990, *The General in His Labyrinth*, while ostensibly concerned with the life of Simón Bolívar and the nineteenth-century wars of liberation in Spanish America, was read by many as García Márquez's guarded epitaph both for Castro himself and for the Cuban revolution—that event that even a decade earlier had still seemed, to so many people between the Rio Grande and Patagonia, to herald a new and better fate for Latin America.

In succeeding, García Márquez's Bolívar also fails. He is trapped by history and by his own character. He is also trapped by time, by the inexorable processes through which even heroism and high ideals become dated. This, perhaps, was the novelist's romantic perspective on the matter. But other, more common-sensical people who had also once supported Castro were speaking in a similar vein in the early nineties. It was not so much that they viewed Castro as an evil tyrant, as people did in Cuban Miami, but rather that he had become for them an anachronism. When, during a state visit to Spain in the summer of 1992 to attend the meeting of Ibero-American heads of state, Castro made a side trip to the Galician village from which his father had emigrated to eastern Cuba almost a century earlier, an embarrassed Spanish socialist accompanying him could not help commenting to a reporter that while Castro had ''once been an inspiration to us, particularly during the time we were struggling against Franco, today he smells of the past. Frankly, the Cuban revolution has been a disappointment.''

This sense that something had gone wrong was shared not only

by European socialists, most of whom had moved a fair distance
to the right during the course of the nineteen-eighties, but to
many in Europe and North America who still considered themselves to be on the left. Even the American writer and filmmaker
Saul Landau, who could claim to know Castro and revolutionary
Cuba intimately and had devoted a lifetime to defending it, sorrowfully admitted to a certain disenchantment. "Cuba," he told
me grimly, over lunch at a Chinese restaurant in Washington, "is
no longer a special place. It's not that I think the government is
going to fall, whatever people in Miami are saying—far from it.
But that doesn't answer the question of what Cuban society is like
today. The mistake people on the left made, I think, was in
imagining that an emancipatory event like the Cuban revolution
was the beginning of a new era—and remember that, whatever
conservatives may say today, that was why radicals in rich countries like the U.S. admired Cuba. It seemed to promise a better
moral life, a fairer life for everyone. But, in retrospect, it now
appears as if the Cuban revolution was not the beginning but
actually the end of something, the last gasp of the Enlightenment.

"Look at Fidel," he continued. "He still believes in reason
and in science. Did you know that every spare moment he has he
spends with the scientists in Cuba's biotechnology research facility? That's why I completely reject your suggestion that Fidel
is a *caudillo*. The *caudillos* were in it for themselves. Fidel is a
patriot, a man almost entirely indifferent to personal comfort, let
alone avid for personal gain. If he can be compared to other
rulers, it would be much more as a prince of the Enlightenment,
and the best analogy might be to Frederick the Great. But,
whether one welcomes the fact or not, today most people, and not
just reactionaries, no longer believe in the things Fidel does.
After Auschwitz and Hiroshima, people in the developed world,
and maybe everywhere else as well, think of reason and science
with great ambivalence. When they employ the terms at all, they
tend to use expressions that are far more mixed, like 'rationalism'
or 'technology.' They suspect the worst of the future; they don't
look forward to it."

"So the Cuban revolution's dream of creating the new man in
a new society is dead?" I asked.

"Maybe all the good dreams are dead," Landau replied, adding, after a short pause, "at least political ones, at least for the moment. Cuba will probably have to participate in the world market whether Fidel Castro stays or goes. Again, the Left's mistake was one of hoping for too much, in this case by imagining that there could be two world markets. While the Soviet Union still existed, and was willing to serve as Cuba's insurance policy against the United States and the worldwide capitalist order, perhaps such an idea was tenable. But, of course, the Soviet Union doesn't exist anymore, the Third World's insurance company is out of business, and as a result countries like Cuba are on their own."

It was odd hearing such an image from Saul Landau, because homespun comparisons between events in business and political ones were such a habitual form of expression in Cuban Miami. A week before, at a conference in Miami on "business opportunities in post-Castro Cuba," I had heard several people say the same thing gloatingly that Landau had expressed with such stony resignation. "Castro's policy has been declared null and void," a Cuban-American tax lawyer told me. "He never expected that the Russians would go belly-up." The implication, of course, was that the time was ripe for a corporate takeover, or a leveraged buyout, of the bankrupt Cuban state. Landau, for his part, hoped that the event could take place peacefully and gradually, and involve the integration of Cuba into the world capitalist economy rather than the overthrow of the regime. Cuban Miami imagined that the two events would go hand in hand. Switching corporate images, the tax lawyer explained, "It's as if the Cuban people had been divided thirty-three years ago between Burger King and McDonald's. But now McDonald's has gone out of business. There is nothing for its customers to do but switch over. If the switch takes place smoothly and without violence, that will be great news for me personally; if it doesn't, I'll get very little satisfaction out of our victory. But the change is coming; there's just no longer any doubt about that."

For the premier defender of Fidel Castro in the United States and a civilized Cuban Miamian of diametrically opposing views to agree about so much testified to just how widespread the expectations were that change was soon coming to Cuba. And Miami, for reasons that were humanly entirely understandable, had taken these expectations and amplified them in 1989 and 1990. By 1990, if possible an even more triumphalist moment in South Florida, they had become all but impossible to rein in. The exile was ending. Even Raul Rodriguez, normally so level-headed, had allowed himself to dream. He had planned, since his first trip back to the island with Ninon in 1980, to return. But now, the political moment seem propitious, and, for Raul, the fact that his son was just reaching the age he had been when the family had left Havana seemed to make such a voyage even more necessary. Raul began to prepare for the trip in earnest. Always obsessed with Cuba, he felt his other interests fade that year as the prospect of return began to mesmerize him. He talked seriously to Ninon and to me of dividing his time between Havana and Miami, and even, if things went well, of opening up a branch of Rodriguez and Quiroga on the island.

A Cuban "we" began to vie for pride of place with the exile "we," the American "we," and the Cuban-American "we" in his conversation. One night, to my stupefaction, I heard him ask a visitor from the island who had come for dinner and debriefing, "Rodolfo, do you really think we should have been in Angola?" The remark had been intended as a reproach, of course, since Raul felt little but loathing for the Cuban expedition to Africa in the seventies. But far more interesting was the degree of identification he felt with it, his sense that in some indefinable way he was as responsible for that military adventure as Americans who had opposed the Vietnam War had felt implicated and shamed, as Americans, by its prosecution. Raul still insisted that he would not simply up and move back to Cuba even if Castro did fall. "I love the Bill of Rights," he liked to say, "and I can't imagine living anywhere without those protections." But, emotionally at least, his bags were packed, not with the shampoo, T-shirts, and aspirins that visitors from the exile carried to their relatives during their one-week reunions, but with the memories of his past and his hopes for the future. The golden purgatory of exile, he thought, might finally be approaching its end.

In the fall of 1991, at the eighth annual awards dinner of FACE, over which, as that organization's president-elect, he had been called upon to preside, Raul allowed himself to give voice in public to the hopes that had been waxing in his mind all year. "Tonight," he told the audience, "FACE pays just tribute to men and women who, through their individual efforts, have so distinguished themselves that they are claimed as examples of the American Dream. More importantly, they are survivors of the Cuban nightmare, a state which has produced two conditions of exile: the exile, first and foremost, of Cuba itself, of its inhabitants who, for the last thirty-two years, have lived isolated from the outside world; second, the exile of those who, like tonight's honorees, have been forced to live outside their homeland. . . . The eyes of the world are upon Cuba again. Everything seems to indicate that the end of both conditions of exile is near. When both conditions of exile end, then the choice to repatriate will be for each one of us to make. When both conditions of exile end, then the choice to emigrate or not will be for each one of them to make. When both conditions of exile end, Alvarez Guedes, Ballet Concerto, Carbonell"—he began to rattle off the names of those FACE was celebrating that evening—"Cidre, Medrano, Piedra, Botifoll, and their compatriots may join in a Cuban renaissance."

In other years, such assertions might have constituted no more than one more expression of *el exilio*'s abiding hope. But in that particular heady moment, so many people got carried away and actually talked themselves into the idea that this year they really would be back in Havana for Christmas. "They were inputting, not processing" was the way that Ninon Rodriguez would later evoke the mind-set of that time. And what exiles had done in 1959, 1960, and 1961, that is, defer purchases and plans on the assumption that the lives they were leading at the moment were not the ones they would soon lead, played itself out, at least among some of the more enthusiastic among them, in 1991 as well. Raul himself lost a small commission as a result of the exile's rekindled hope. One afternoon, I went to pick him up at his office in Coral Gables, and he greeted me with a shake of his head and the information that an addition he had been scheduled to do on the house of a local doctor had just been canceled. It seemed the man had called to say that he could no longer afford to have the work done. When Raul had asked why, he had replied, as if it had been the most obvious thing in the world, that he needed to save all the capital he could so that he would have enough on hand to start a branch of his practice—and Raul Rodriguez, perhaps despite himself, smiled as he quoted the line—"next year in Havana."

Raul did not go so far as to say that the man's behavior was typical, but it was hardly exceptional either. "You have to know," he told me, "that a lot of people here are preparing for the day. I'm not so much talking about the political people, particularly in the Foundation. Sometimes I think those debates are more about the future of power in Miami than about politics in a post-Castro Cuba. No, I mean you have all these groups like the Sugar Growers, the Industrialists, all the old trade associations. And then there are labor groups. My barber in Coral Gables still pays his union dues, and he told me the other day, 'Raul, they finally might be worth something.' You have lawyers studying the pre-Castro penal code, and other people just wondering what happened to their parents' houses. Everything has shaken loose. It's hard to know what people expect to happen, or how the change will actually take place, but they feel—I feel it too—that there's finally a chance."

In fairness to Raul, he was one of the few people I met in Cuban Miami that year who entertained hopes of returning to Cuba, of participating in what liberals and conservatives among the exiles alike were referring to as "national reconciliation," while maintaining at least a measure of skepticism even about his own emotions. In the original draft of his FACE address, Raul had written of the evening's honorees that they "will join in a Cuban renaissance." By the time he delivered it, he had substituted the word "may." And the ensuing year would demonstrate that his caution had been amply justified. For all the hope of Castro falling, Castro had not fallen; for all the talk of return that had circulated in the exile, the Cubans were still in Miami that next Christmas, not in Havana. Indeed, if there had been any change in the situation, it was that increasing numbers of Cubans from the island were arriving in Miami. Some came on rafts and inner tubes, the so-called *balseros,* or "rafters," who left coastal Cuban towns like Santa Fe late at night and took their chances in the Florida Strait. Others came from the population, most of it elderly, that Castro allowed to travel to see relatives in Miami, and who chose not to return. Cuba was not being freed, but, rather, the exile was being reinforced.

Eventually, the excitement over an imminent return quieted down. No one had dreamed it would take this long for "Castro's final hour" to elapse. Before too long, even the Calle Ocho broadsheets, those perennial founts of optimism, hope, and verticality, seemed to lose their taste for running banner headlines that proclaimed, "We've Won," and that had been such a feature of the issues printed in 1990 and 1991. And the bumper stickers that had enjoyed such a vogue in Cuban Miami during that same period, particularly those that took the change in the relations of force between Miami and Havana for granted, and even boasted, "The Only Dialogue We Want with Castro: Do You Want a Blindfold, Yes or No?," had begun to look far more like relics than the regime supposedly already resting on history's dustbin. And as a result, some older complaints, long suppressed or, at least, long tamped down, within *el exilio* once again had begun resurfacing. Prominent among them, for all the fervent insistence, within Cuban Miami as much as if not more than outside of it, that the Cubans in South Florida epitomized the American Dream, was a rekindled anger toward the United States itself, a feeling that had never entirely left many exiles since the American betrayal of *la causa* at the Bay of Pigs, when, instead of sending in the U.S. Marines, the Kennedy administration had left Brigade 2506 to be killed or captured. The betrayal that the Kennedy-Khrushchev accord the following year that ended the Cuban Missile crisis represented for the exile only embedded still further in the psyche of Miami Cubans the belief that they had been duped, and probably were continuing to be duped, by an ungrateful and two-faced American establishment.

As a result, in 1992, Miami too had entered its own metaphoric version of the regimen the Castro regime had imposed on the island the previous year and referred to as "the special period in time of peace." Both were, in their disparate ways, responses to the failure of history to behave as it had been supposed to. Instead of giving birth to the new man, revolutionary Cuba, which had once boasted that it was "the first free territory of the Americas," was reduced to distributing bicycles to its population, cutting off electricity to parts of the cities on a regular basis to save fuel, and daubing the walls of public spaces with slogans like "Socialism or Death" and "Our Revolution: An Eternal Baraguá." In an era when Communism had collapsed, the notion of choosing between a system that was defunct almost everywhere else in the world and death could not but be menacing, while the reference to Baraguá—an episode during the Ten Years' War of Cuban Independence when a nineteenth-century revolutionary hero, the black general Antonio Maceo, had refused to surrender to the Spanish army surrounding his own—was almost as dire.

Fidel Castro had urged the Cuban people not to despair, and assured them that if they could weather the difficult year or two that was in store for them things would improve. And although the comparisons that outsiders hostile to Cuban Miami liked to make between the rhetoric of the exile and that of the regime on the island were often overdrawn, it was undeniable that in 1992 what resemblances did exist were all too easily observable. Officials of the Cuban-American National Foundation insisting over and over again in speeches and interviews that 1992 and 1993 would be the years of decision, the talk on the Calle Ocho radio stations imploring Cuban-Americans to maintain their cohesion, an orchestrated campaign against dissenters in Miami, and a redoubled effort to lobby both the U.S. and foreign governments to get tougher with Castro—these were only some of the examples of a mobilization among South Florida Cuban refugees at a level not seen for at least fifteen years. It was a time when a hundred thousand signatures were collected demanding that the American government interpret the U.S. Neutrality Act in such a way that it would not bar, as it was clearly meant to, Cuban exiles from mounting military operations against Cuba from U.S. soil. The petitions were delivered to the White House by descendants, now resident in Miami, of two heroes of Cuba's wars of independence, Andres Vargas Gomez, the grandson of General Máximo Gómez, and Enrique Maceo, the grandson of General Antonio Maceo.

And when the American administration rejected these demands, and it was even reported that U.S. intelligence officials had cooperated with their Cuban opposite numbers during the Pan-American Games that had been held in Havana in the summer of 1991, the anger of Miami was as deep as its expectations had been high. It was an old trajectory in Cuban history. "Poor Cuba," wrote the influential nineteenth-century Cuban historian Luis Estévez y Romero, "always hopeful, always disappointed." He might have added "and always ambivalent toward the United States," an attitude that was as applicable in 1992 in Miami as it was when Estévez wrote his great book on Cuban society, *Desde el Zanjón hasta Baire,* in the late eighteen-nineties.

The anger toward the *Herald* had been part of this ambivalence. It not only reflected the desire of many people in Cuban Miami to find someone to blame for the fact that Fidel Castro had not yet fallen—a tendency in Cuban political thinking that many Cuban writers, from the historian Luis Aguilar Leon to writers like Guillermo Cabrera Infante, never stopped ruefully pointing out—but played on the deeper bitterness over the betrayal at the Bay of Pigs as well. What people in Miami accused the newspaper of having done, after all, was more than simply having printed inaccurate and biased stories. That would have been bad enough, but, as Jorge Mas Canosa had put it, the *Herald* had done more. It had, he said, betrayed the "ideals" of the exile, by which he meant above all the "ideal" of the liberation of Cuba, the "ideal" of return. Once again, Cuban Miami's newest complaint seemed to recapitulate its oldest one. In accusing the *Herald* of having betrayed *la causa* in 1992 through distortion and indifference, there was an echo of the great betrayals of 1961 and 1962 that was inescapable to anyone who knew any history. In a sense, the correct interpretation of the signs on Miami city buses reading "I don't believe *The Miami Herald*" was "We Cuban exiles don't believe the United States, and we have good reasons to feel that way."

The problem, as far as relations between Cubans and non-Cubans in Miami were concerned, was that few non-Cubans did know any history, or, at the very least, that few were willing to take what they knew into account when thinking about the *Herald* controversy. To Miami liberals, the Cubans were right-wing ya-hoos trying to abrogate the First Amendment. To other non-Cuban South Floridians, they were simply pushy immigrants who not only had done well, but now wanted to control what was said about them as well. Cuban demands for the imposition of a kind of linguistic martial law, particularly when they seemed to carry the blessing of Miami's mayor, made such fears appear well founded, but, once again, the problem was that Cuban Miami saw itself in large measure as a community of exiles, while for non-Cuban Miami such an assertion was almost entirely myste-rious. Wasn't America about fresh starts? To which, predictably, many exiles would have replied, had the question been posed to them directly, "Perhaps, but exile is about remembering."

And further complicating matters was the fact that what Cu-bans in South Florida said they felt was only part of what they actually felt. On the surface, what was most evident about Mi-ami, for all the conflicts between Cubans and non-Cubans, was all the nationalist noise. There can be few places in the United States where there is more waving of the American flag, both metaphorically and literally, and few places where the rituals of patriotic observance are carried out with more fervor and punc-tilio. To watch a mostly Cuban-American crowd at a Miami Heat basketball game or at an event at the Orange Bowl or at the new Joe Robbie Stadium in North Miami belting out "The Star-Spangled Banner" was to witness what appeared on the surface like the most old-fashioned, fervent expression of immigrant pa-triotism. And to a large degree, particularly among younger Cu-ban Miamians, that was exactly what it was. For others, and not simply those who belonged to Raul and Ninon Rodriguez's gen-eration or their elders, the story was, for better or worse, more complicated. When they sang the American national anthem, they could not help hearing the Cuban one inside their heads as well. They might revel in Francis Scott Key's evocation of the (American) flag still flying after a night of bombardment, but, at least contrapuntally, they were also stirred by the words of Perucho Figueredo's anthem with its call:

> To the battle, Bayameses!
> Let the fatherland proudly observe you!
> Do not fear a glorious death,
> To die for the fatherland is to live!

The result, unsurprisingly, was a degree of symbolic confusion in Cuban Miami that was all but impossible to untangle. For not only were Cuban Miamians, however much they might insist that they were not immigrants, not yet anyway, attached to the symbols of the U.S.A., but even the symbols of *exile* patriotism, from which one might have expected American icons to be wholly absent, often were brandished in tandem with the Stars and Stripes. Mas Canosa's organization was emblematic in this regard. It was the Cuban-*American* National Foundation, not the Cuban National Foundation, even though fund-raising brochures addressed to prospective members—who were referred to in them as "esteemed compatriots," a phrase that does not seem to admit the notion of dual allegiance—spoke of the Foundation as "the crucible of all the ideals and love of all Cubans [who aspire to serve our] great nation," and as "one big family" sharing a "historic responsibility." And even the weekend warriors, whom the fall of the Berlin Wall had been drawing in steadily increasing numbers to Alpha 66's training camps in the Florida Everglades, were often photographed with their color guard, which proudly displayed the flags of both Cuba and the United States. Indeed, the pairing was so familiar that when, in the winter of 1992, *The Miami Herald* ran a front-page picture of such a unit, no one I met in Miami, including the many people who complained bitterly about the existence of the training camps, seemed to find the image of this binational guerrilla army worth a moment's passing comment.

But for all the flag (or, more exactly, flags) waving, this easy movement in Cuban Miami between American and Cuban patriotism concealed as much as if not more than it disclosed. When Luis Botifoll insisted to me that he loved the United States, even though he would have preferred the chance to live out his life in Havana; or when Sandra Oldham spoke of her desire to reassure me that she, too, loved America, even though she was still trying to come to terms with her parents' having been forced to flee the island; or even when Raul Rodriguez, echoing this same informal pledge of allegiance, albeit far more warmly, talked of how uncomfortable he felt during any sporting event that pitted the U.S. against Cuba, because he loved both countries so passionately and thus did not know for which he should cheer; they were expressing only one acceptable, relatively benign portion of the exile's mixed and uncomfortable feelings about being in America to begin with, about the relationship they had enjoyed with the country as exiles over the past thirty-three years, and, most disturbingly of all, about the feelings toward the U.S. that they harbored as Cubans—feelings that long antedated the rise of Fidel Castro and that were by no means as positive as all the pro-American verbiage in Cuban Miami might have led an unwary outsider to expect.

Non-Cuban liberals in Miami tended, if anything, to be appalled by a crude, old-fashioned American patriotism among the exiles that they associated with the worst excesses of Ronald Reagan. But although it was true that Cuban-Americans had become the staunchest of Republicans in Dade County, the reasons for this had as much to do with Fidel Castro, and, for that matter, with the betrayal of *la causa* by John F. Kennedy's Democratic White House, than with any inherent Cuban predilection for the Right. Pre-Castro Cuba had boasted of a far greater diversity of political opinion than the United States during the same period, however rarely the dictators who had ruled the island, from Machado to Batista, had permitted the adherents of these various tendencies to participate in political life. American right-wing superpatriotism might have been a natural home for the Batistano royalists who formed so large a part of the first wave of Cuban refugees in 1959 and 1960, but the tragedy of Cuba had been that this group was soon joined by hundreds of thousands of people, the vast majority of whom had been either liberals or leftists, many of whom had even supported Fidel Castro for a time. They were socialists and Christian democrats, members of the Ortodoxo party and former members of Castro's 26th of July movement. In the mid-eighties, the exile cinematographer and filmmaker Nestor Almendros even discovered several of the founders of the Communist party of Cuba living in exile in the working-class Miami suburb of Hialeah. They were, predictably, bitterly anti-Castro, but hardly in the way that Republican party activists in South Florida, or members of the Cuban-American National Foundation, might have wished.

As Raul Rodriguez often said, "We in the exile went right because when we arrived in this country, we soon discovered that the liberals and the Left here were pro-Castro. No matter what we told them about abuses at home, they refused to believe us. We were all Batistanos, all pigs and fascists. The only people who would listen, at least after 1962, were the Republicans, I'm sorry to say. You could look at what happened in Miami as a kind of protective coloration. It was partly a reaction by people who had suffered, the idea that the enemy of your enemy is your friend. And later, I think, this right-wing attitude came from the fact that the Republicans were in the White House, in power, for so long. People here felt beleaguered. They didn't want an enemy in Washington as well as one in Havana, and although, personally, I'm a Democrat, I'm not about to fault them for the choice they made.

"Besides," he continued, "they had real reasons as well as emotional ones for not trusting liberals, locally, nationally, or internationally." He paused, and, smiling, said, "*Yo no creo en el* Herald," "I don't believe in the *Herald*." "That's the mood here. People get fixed in a certain mind-set. They remember when no one would listen, when in New York and Washington people were pretty quick on the draw, awfully ready to dismiss our pain and our suffering almost as if we'd had it coming. So you shouldn't be surprised that Cubans today here in Miami are still very suspicious. They remember when the Democrats never spared them a second thought. It's not true anymore, but in the same way that people still haven't forgiven the *Herald* for its behavior when Ramon Mestre chained himself to the front door of the paper, and forget he now helps run the paper, they also forget that things have changed in the U.S. since a lot of these political decisions were first made.''

In this move to the right, however, older traditions of U.S.-Cuban rivalry and, to put the matter more starkly, U.S.-Cuban antipathy had not disappeared entirely, but rather had only gone underground. ''Only Cubans and Mexicans,'' said Pedro Freyre, a Miami lawyer who had been a classmate of Raul's at the University of Miami, gone on to represent Dow Corning in Latin America, and now ran an insurance firm, ''have such triumphantly mixed feelings about the United States. It's not a simple matter of anti-Americanism. The cultures are too close for that, despite all the ways in which both Cubans and Americans have historically insisted that they differed. Anyhow, three countries where the national sport is baseball in a world where everyone else, practically, plays soccer are bound to feel a certain affinity. But, all joking aside, Cubans and Americans may go back a long way; they may understand each other; Teddy Roosevelt may have ridden up San Juan Hill, and José Martí proclaimed Cuban independence from exile in the U.S.; but on the Cuban side particularly, there has always been as much hostility as there was warmth.''

What Freyre was alluding to was almost exactly the same bill of particulars that all Cuban patriots since José Martí had laid at America's door. It had been Martí, after all, not Fidel Castro, who had written in the last letter before his death that ''it is my duty to prevent, through the independence of Cuba, the U.S.A. from spreading over the West Indies and falling with added weight upon other lands of our America. . . . I know the monster, because I have lived in its lair—and my weapon is only the slingshot of David.'' And Martí was a hero in Cuban Miami—his image was ubiquitous in the offices of Eighth Street radio station managers and officials of political exile groupings. Even to pretend that these words were an aberration, or, as was more commonly the case, to try to ignore them, was bound to be difficult at any moment. But at a time when the strains between the exile and the larger society in which it found itself were beginning once again to show, it was only to be expected that people who considered themselves to be Cuban patriots would not be able to buffer themselves entirely from anti-Americanism, a feeling that was one of the most important constituent parts historically of that Cuban patriotism. The exile resented having to be in America, but intellectually the resentment toward America predated the exile. And if this feeling was quiescent in Miami most of the time, that was due as much as anything to the fact that the language of anti-Americanism had been poisoned by Fidel Castro—a case, once more, of the enemy of one's enemy being one's friend.

But that friend had once been an enemy, and there were many people in Miami who remembered the fact, however quietly they kept the news. What non-Cubans mistook for Cuban arrogance was, as often as not, Cuban ambivalence. And the leading families of the exile, as Ninon Rodriguez sometimes called them, were in many cases descended from the Creole families whose sons had been prominent in all Cuba's wars of independence. If Fidel Castro had hijacked anti-Americanism, this did not mean that they had forgotten all the injustices of American policy toward Cuba, from the U.S. refusal to intervene in the nineteenth century to its decision to virtually annex Cuba for a generation after the Spanish-American War. An exile that considered itself nationalist was an exile that would, from time to time anyway, be drawn to anti-Americanism. It might be a passion that dared not speak its name, a subtext to other controversies, but in 1992, in Cuban Miami, it lurked not too far beneath the surface. To honor Martí, to contribute to the restoration of the San Carlos Theater in Key West from which Cuban independence had been proclaimed in 1898, to evoke the other great figures of Cuban independence—Varela, Céspedes, Saco, and the others—was, wittingly or not, to traffic in at least a species of anti-Americanism. All the flag waving in the world could not change this.

This was at the root of *el exilio*'s stiff-necked attitude toward the United States. It might come clothed in the fashionable language of cultural diversity—as when Xavier Suarez had attacked the American press for presuming that its own traditions were superior to those of other countries. It might even borrow the language of the civil rights movement, as when, one evening, a young Cuban-American doctor named Gloria Sanchez told me angrily that "we Cubans don't have to assimilate. Martin Luther King made that possible for us." And, no doubt, since Miami Cubans were no more immune to the tendencies in the larger American culture that emphasized multiculturalism, or, more importantly, a certain cult of victimization, these assertions were sincere. But they were not the crux of the matter. As always, that was to be found in *el tema* itself, in the explosive mixture of obsession, pain, and wounded pride with which the exile had been coping for thirty-three years and with which, the optimistic predictions of 1990 and 1991 to the contrary notwithstanding, it was likely to have to go on confronting from north of the Florida Strait for so much longer than it had anticipated.

7

It WAS PRECISELY the exile's abiding experience of defeat, its embittered familiarity with cycle after cycle of hopes raised only to be dashed, far more than whatever degree of economic success it had wrested for itself in Dade County or its sense of being culturally at ease there, that really accounted for the central role Miami continued to play in the imaginations of Cuban refugees, their children, and their grandchildren, whether or not they actually chose to live in the city. After all, for all the political passions that had swept Miami since Cuban refugees first began arriving there in 1959, almost every one of the exile's organized ventures, from 1959 until the collapse of the Soviet empire, and whether military or political, had ended in failure. Hard-line Cuban Miamians might take comfort from the fact that, from Vietnam to Nicaragua, Cuban-Americans had helped fight, and, according to some, win, the Cold War. One of their number, Felix Rodriguez, had become a career CIA officer, and could boast of having helped capture Che Guevara in the Bolivian altiplano in 1967 and of organizing the resupply of the Nicaraguan Contras in the mid-nineteen-eighties. But even Rodriguez, in his memoir, *Shadow Warrior,* conceded a certain feeling of frustration. "Sometimes I feel a bit like Ulysses," he wrote. "Like him, I am from an island nation. Like him, I went to war. And like him, I am having a hard time getting home."

Despite Rodriguez's military exploits, and Jorge Mas Canosa's lobbying, the political importance to the Republican party of

Cuban-American voters, and, for that matter, their readiness to contribute to the coffers of Democratic politicians like Congressman Torricelli who were ready to support their cause, the exile had little to show for its efforts. Mas Canosa might be received by Yeltsin, and candidates for high office in the United States might bend over backwards demonstrating their support for legislation like the Cuban Democracy Act, but the fact remained that Fidel Castro was still in Havana and the exile could still not go home. Whatever the degree of Cuban self-absorption—and it was so celebrated among Cubans themselves that there was even a well-known term for it, *el ombliguismo de Cuba,* roughly translated, "the sense of Cuba as being the navel of the universe," an idea whose history can be traced back to José Martí himself—most exiles, even at their most grandiloquent, understood perfectly well that they belonged to a small diaspora whose claims were unlikely to be taken seriously all that much longer in a world increasingly used to far larger historical injustices than the one *el exilio* had suffered. But if they could not command the attention of the world outside Miami for very long, at least they could make *el tema* the theme of the city as a whole. And in establishing in Miami a simulacrum convincing both to themselves and to outsiders of the Cuba they had lost, the exiles could demonstrate that theirs was not solely a story of defeat. They had won somewhere, if only by virtue of having remade a mid-sized city on the southeastern edge of the United States in their own image.

This was more than braggadocio. To be sure, things had changed in Miami. New immigrants from Central America and the Caribbean meant that the city was no longer simply a place that could be described in terms of its Cuban population and of native-born Americans, both black and white. Moreover, if the identity of Cubans as new arrivals was now outmoded, their homogeneity as a culture was threatened by burgeoning rates of intermarriage with the group Florida demographers referred to as non-Cuban whites, as well as by the attraction American culture held for the younger generations of Cuban-Americans. Nonetheless, if it was now possible for Cubans who had grown up in

Miami during the sixties and seventies to wax nostalgic for *el Miami de ayer,* and to recall fondly when East Little Havana had been a Cuban neighborhood rather than a Nicaraguan one, the fact remained that their attachment to the city, their sense of its being their only haven in the world, had, if anything, only grown stronger as the gulf widened between their dreams of return and the likelihood of their exile continuing for a long time.

Many things contributed to this Miami effect. The names of the supermarkets, of the small grocery stores and the funeral homes, helped keep the Cuban past alive in the mind of the exile. There was a supermarket chain called Varadero, there were any number of cafeterias called Flor de Camagüey, "Flower of Camagüey," or the Pearl of the Antilles, which had been Columbus's name for Cuba, and there was even La Habana Vieja, "Old Havana." This last, a restaurant, was decorated with the street names of intra-mural Havana and murals of the city drawn on the walls. One ate one's *lechón asado* under a sign reading Obispo Street. It was the restaurant as theme park; the theme park as *memento mori*. Some businesses had simply been started up by their exiled owners in Miami once again, and these were often graced by signs marking their original date of establishment in Cuba in the nineteenth century rather than their reestablishment in South Florida in the latter half of the twentieth. And if, these days, increasing num-bers of young Cuban-Americans preferred for the most part to eat at the local McDonald's than at the Versailles, this did not render the existence of this archetypal Miami cafeteria any less impor-tant psychologically. Older, more established American immi-grant groups have felt the same way. It is common, after all, to go to what still remains of Italian inner-city neighborhoods in the American Northeast and Midwest and find the tables in the local restaurants filled with Italian-American couples who moved to the suburbs long ago, but are drawn back to the old neighborhood for the reassuring smells and tastes of childhood. And they can go home again, whether to Brooklyn or to Sicily. In the Cuban case, a restaurant like the Versailles had to do double duty, simulta-neously evoking the past and existing as its only tangible trace.

When the Foundation's Rene Silva had insisted that "here in

Miami, Cuba both lives and is reborn every day, just like the sun, in its exiled children,'' he was doubtless overstating the case, since many of the exiled children in question were, at any given moment, at least as likely to be pondering the question of whether or not the Miami Hurricanes were likely to repeat as national collegiate football champions as they were the problem of whether they would be free to return to Havana. But even among the more assimilated young Cuban-Americans—those who lived in South Florida, anyway; those who had moved elsewhere were another matter—people for whom all the talk of *el tema* that they heard from their parents and grandparents was more of an imposition than an emotional catharsis bonding one generation to another, there was a ready consensus that Miami was not like the rest of the United States, that it was, in the literal sense of the word, essentially Cuban, and that, whatever the political future of the island, the three decades-long struggle on the part of the exile to create a civic environment in which the memories of the Cuban past would not easily fade and the customs of pre-Castro Havana would continue to seem relevant made it a virtual certainty that *la Cuba de ayer* would go on existing, if only in this re-created form, north of the Florida Strait and south of Fort Lauderdale.

Cuban Miamians were justly proud of the accomplishment, but to an outsider what was almost as arresting about the simulacrum they had fashioned was what they had excluded from it. For if this was the Cuba of yesterday, it was a sanitized, folkloric version of that city. Those who had loved Havana in the fifties for its dazzling literary life, the baroque inventiveness of even quite ordinary middle-class table talk, and a sensuality heavily infused with African and homosexual overtones would have found little on the surface of life in Miami to remind them of any of these elements. Not that they did not continue to exist in secret. Cuban Miami remained almost as gay a place as Havana had been, but no one admitted to the fact, as the rates of female HIV infection—accounted for by many epidemiologists as having been spread to wives from husbands who had covert relations with boys and then went home and had unprotected sex—attested. As for culture,

Cuban Miami was proud of its writers, but, as if by tacit agreement, the community honored the artists and the artists chose to
live elsewhere—an arrangement that seemed to satisfy both sides.
Only the painters, drawn to South Florida as much if not more by
the tropical light as by the Cubanity of Dade County, were an
exception to the rule.

It was as if the complexity of prerevolutionary Havana culture
was too much to bear, just as the complexity and, more importantly, the contradictions within prerevolutionary Cuban society
had to be glossed over if the exile was to maintain its coherence.
Cubans, in the canonical Miami version, had gotten along before
Fidel Castro. To believe otherwise meant sanctioning the thought
that the tyrant's downfall might not guarantee that they would get
along in the future. By the same token, to represent in Miami
pre-1959 Cuban art and literature in all its depth might mean
letting the message of that art register its discordant note. It was,
for example, commonplace to hear the writer Virgilio Piñera
extolled in Miami. Such praise made sense, since Piñera, who
had remained in Havana long after most of the other writers of his
generation had gone into exile, had been hounded into an early
grave by Castro's cultural commissars. And yet Piñera's work, as
opposed to his political stance or his status as a martyr, was much
more complicated. His Havana was no splendid city of columns,
as another great writer, the Castro loyalist Alejo Carpentier, had
dubbed it. Instead, his Cuba, long before the triumph of Communism, had been "a jail, from which no one can escape." As
the critic Carlos Luis once wrote, Piñera was Cuban literature's
bad conscience, a writer who refused to see his country through
contented eyes. But Miami, beleaguered, vertical Miami, could
not hear such a message, and, by and large, rejected it.

The Cubanness of the exile was a Cubanness radically cut
back, by those who had been most instrumental in preserving it,
in much the same way that a gardener cuts back a plant when the
water supply is too limited to nourish a full canopy of leaves and
new stems. The old Havana had been cosmopolitan; indeed, so-
phistication had been its signature, whether intellectual, sexual,
or aesthetic. But all cosmopolitanism encourages ambivalence

not fidelity, a sense of the world as a single entity rather than a fantasy of national uniqueness, self-doubt rather than hope, eccentricity rather than community. Ramon Puig's *guayabera* shop might boast a mural of prerevolutionary Havana, complete with images of the famous eccentrics of the period, behind the cash register and beside framed pictures of Oliver North, Jorge Mas Canosa, and the Argentine comedian Porcel, but a community at war could ill afford eccentricity, or, at least, that was the majority opinion within the exile. Instead, people craved a simple, reduced Cuban culture, one based on shared memories, similar tastes in food and music, and a notion of what Cubans "were like." "[We Cubans] are here together with our music and our food," a businessman named Leslie Pantin, Jr., who was the principal organizer of the annual Calle Ocho carnival, once told me, in an effort to explain what was special about Miami for the exile. And there was no doubt that this reassuring version of Cubanity, with all the kinks hidden from view, was more in line with what the community craved than anything more challenging. And why not? Cuban Miami had been challenged enough for thirty-three years. If it wanted anything from its culture, it was balm, not fresh abrasions.

This was why when Cuban Miamians talked about what was special about the city, they were most often describing an idealized family writ large. The stories they had told themselves about Cuba over the decades had grown increasingly mythical, increasingly detached from reality, the longer the separation had persisted. Cuba had been one kind of place, just as Miami was one kind of place. This view had an interesting pedigree. On the face of things, of course, there is no reason why people who had grown up rich in Miramar in the forties or fifties should have agreed about the nature of Cubanness with people who had grown up poor in Santiago de Cuba a decade or two later. Indeed, there was no reason that people who had grown up in the rich quarters of Havana and others who had been born in the city's slums in the same period should have been able to agree any more readily than someone who grew up in Beverly Hills, California, is likely to agree with someone who grew up in South Central about the true essence of Los Angeles. And yet what was remarkable about Miami was the degree of consensus that did exist in the city about what the Cuba of yesterday had been like. That there was a certain reluctance to differ about Miami was understandable. After all, whatever separated the exiles, feeling under assault from the island and misunderstood in the United States made them likely to present a common front to the outside world. But rewriting the past was another matter.

Few Cuban Miamians were willing to admit that a rewriting had taken place. When pressed, some said that these were matters that, like the question of whether the Miami community was an exile or an immigration, had to wait for a post-Castro Cuba to come into being before they could be settled. "You want me to criticize my memories," a friend of Raul Rodriguez's once said to me, "and I love my memories. I cherish them. They're all I have of Cuba." And when I suggested that if these memories were false, then the disappointment that Miami Cubans would feel when they actually did get to go back would be boundless, I was met with a blank stare and a grimly pious hope. "We're all Cubans. We'll learn to understand each other again."

But the distortions of memory, like the contradictions between the Cubans of the Miami diaspora and the Cubans who had remained on the island, were not, whatever most people in *el exilio* might believe, simply a function of Fidel Castro's government. There had been a few moments in the history of the exile when people had been forced to confront this fact, most notably during the Mariel boatlift. For what Mariel revealed to people in Miami was something that they had either forgotten or chosen to repress from their memories about what Cuba was like—that Cubans were not mostly white, like Cuban exiles, but that the island had always been heavily black and mulatto, and, with the flight of almost fifty percent of the pre-1959 white population, and a higher birth rate among Cuban blacks than the Cuban whites who had remained, the proportion was now about thirty percent white and about seventy percent black and mulatto. But once the Marielitos had been absorbed into the exile population, it was as if Cuban Miami began to forget even this simple fact about its lost homeland. Ten years later, when Raul Rodriguez would show the slides he had taken of Havana, it was common to hear people he had invited exclaim at the number of black faces they saw in the pictures, or murmur unhappily about a plot by Fidel Castro to repopulate Havana with nonwhites.

And so, probably not surprisingly, the one person I met during the time I lived in Miami who was fully alive to the distortions about life in Cuba that exile had imposed was a black Cuban, a former builder and now a vice-president of the local chapter of the United Way named David Rosemond. As the name suggested, Rosemond's family had originally come from the French West Indies. His paternal grandfather had gone from Martinique to Panama, where he had labored on the canal just after the turn of the century. There, he had met David's grandmother, who was from Jamaica. Hearing of opportunities in Cuba, they had immigrated to the island in 1910, and settled in Havana. In a sense, although there were few Cuban blacks in Miami, Rosemond's background was typical. His father, he was quick to tell me, "believed that leaving Cuba was the worst thing in the world," and tended to blame everything that had changed on the island, every fissure between Miami and Havana, on Fidel Castro. And it was clear, after an hour in Rosemond's company, that he, too, loved Cuba fiercely and hungered to return, but that unlike his father he saw how partial the picture of *la Cuba de ayer* to which Miami subscribed really was.

What Rosemond wanted to talk about was sociology, not emotional rescue. "The first thing you have to see," he told me, "is how powerful this selective memory in Miami can be. I know many people who were dirt poor in Cuba, and who came here and did well, who have totally blocked the idea that they were ever needy in Cuba. I remember one woman who I know for a fact used to eke out a living taking in laundry in Havana—I know because in the old days my mom used to help her out when she could—and now that she's doing well here talks about herself in Cuba as if she had belonged to a family of sugar mill owners. And, of course, I and my family don't say anything. But I can't help feeling that if this woman could go back to Cuba, the way someone who comes from the Dominican Republic or Jamaica can go back, she would realize, 'No, I made my way in the U.S. If I'd stayed in Cuba, I'd probably still be poor.' But of course she can't go back and these kinds of myths acquire a life of their own.''

I asked Rosemond why he thought that the poorer refugees who had followed their more well-heeled counterparts into exile after 1964 hadn't brought with them a countermyth that, at the very least, might have coexisted in Miami with the benign, official version, and, possibly modified it. But he only shook his head.

''By the time other groups of Cubans arrived, it was too late,'' he said. ''It was all a question of timing and of the enclosed quality of this community. Because the early refugees tended to be upper class, they were the ones who got to shape the myths of our exile. And because the version they offer is pleasant—no, more than pleasant, consoling, beautiful—everyone subscribes to it. Besides, it was the wealthy who set the cultural parameters, and many peoples, not just Cubans, have a tendency to emulate the wealthy. In our case, following the pattern set by a Cuban rich class was a way of resisting the United States, a reflection of the exile's desire to remain culturally intact, even if that version of our culture isn't entirely accurate as a rendering. We have a saying in Miami about the prototypical exile that 'his watch stopped in 1959.' But it's even more complicated than that, because a lot of people's watches stopped in 1959 in Miramar or Vedado even though in those days they wouldn't have been allowed inside the Vedado Tennis Club under any circumstances.''

Rosemond repeated several times during the time I spent with him how much he regretted these distortions. ''We're joined together here in Miami in this mirage. In accepting this, we've forfeited our own authentic experience. Once you leave Ha . . . Miami—I almost said Havana, didn't I?—you realize how ridiculous this can seem to outsiders. I remember meeting some Puerto Rican students when I was at the University of Florida who kept asking how every Cuban they ever met could come from Havana. 'The city doesn't look very big on a map,' one of

them told me, 'so we figure it must have had a couple of floors.'
You get the idea. But more seriously, as a black man I'm constantly aware here of how hard it is to get my fellow Cubans to
accept the country's black heritage. There's a distortion of memory, but there's also a 'bleaching' of it. To give you a trivial
example, I like to dance, and I'm constantly meeting Cubans who
say, 'Oh, that's because you're black.' And I always reply, 'No,
it's because I'm Cuban. If we still lived on the island, you'd
know that.''

In the end, however, Rosemond was more inclined to understand than to condemn. ''What explains Miami,'' he told me
toward the end of our lunch, ''is people's need to defend themselves psychologically. The copying of upper-class manners can
be traced to this. After all, my parents' generation were horrified
by the sexual permissiveness they found in the United States—
there was even a myth circulating in some Miami homes in the
sixties that American doctors removed girl's hymens, so that
virginity couldn't be established, almost as if there had been a
mandate from the state that people be sexually loose. So the style
of the Havana upper class, with its rigid separation of women into
good girls and whores, wives and mistresses, seemed like a way
of defending the family, even though the chaperone, which became ubiquitous in Miami through the mid-seventies, was completely an upper-class phenomenon back in Cuba. And our need
to think we were all the same was a way of unifying against
Castro too. The Cuban Communists didn't seem to be divided,
and I believe that, unconsciously anyway, a lot of people here,
including some who remember a lot more accurately than they
like to let on, felt that we could not afford to be either, even if that
meant a certain amount of thinking and even remembering in
lockstep. If we wanted to survive—and we did, and we have—we
had to stay almost as vertical with regard to the past as we did
with regard to Communism on the island.''

What Rosemond did insist on, no matter how ironic his take on
the historic reasons for Miami's lapses of memory, was that this
strain of conformity would serve the community less well in the
future than it had in the past. ''Look,'' he said, ''I love my dad

and I know he's an intelligent man. So when he says to me on a hot day in Miami that it was never this hot in Cuba, or that the meat tasted better there, I know that he is well aware that the meat probably tasted better because we got it freshly butchered, straight from the farm, not because Cuban meat was naturally better than U.S. meat. But as long as we are in exile, that's another one of the psychological defenses I was talking about. But what happens when we do go back, when we discover that meat is meat and a hot day in the tropics is a hot day in the tropics? Worse, what happens when we discover that all the possessions we have worked so hard to accumulate here in Miami actually have the effect of separating us from our fellow Cubans on the island? Historically, Cubans have a bad habit of blaming others for everything bad that happens to them. And since we do have reason to blame Castro, that tendency has only grown worse with exile. The Cuban community, I fear—and I'm a person who doesn't plan to go back to Cuba to live, but would like to use my skills to help rebuild the island—will be disappointed, and blaming the discrepancy between what they imagined and what Cuba's actually like won't work for long."

And yet Rosemond was not optimistic that habits of feeling and reacting that had developed over the hard course of exile could be easily transformed. "It's a difficult situation to confront," he told me as we parted. "Most people here get their information from the Cuban radio, or the *Herald*, or, most of all, from the representations of the past that they get from their families. And since they can't check the facts, they're left with their feelings, their passionate, unreliable feelings. A lot of the time, younger people snicker when they hear their parents on *el tema*. They wink at each other, and say, 'Oh, here they go again.' But the truth is that these are the only versions of the truth they know, and while hearing this kind of talk all the time may be exasperating, you shouldn't underestimate how reassuring it is as well."

The proof of what David Rosemond had said was everywhere. Armed with these generic family accounts, young Cuban-Americans could leave Miami to go to school and still thirst to return—a homesickness squared or cubed by exile. And when they did return, or when they came to Miami from elsewhere in the United States, or from Spain, or Venezuela, or wherever else there were outposts of the Cuban diaspora, many felt just as much at home as these family stories they had heard all their lives had made them expect they would. "Of course I felt at home here right away," a young professor at Florida International University named Dario Moreno told me laughingly over drinks in Coral Gables. "From the moment I arrived, I knew I had returned to the Cuba that my parents had always described to me when I was a kid growing up in Los Angeles. They always talked about Cuba with such love that anyone would have had to be completely heartless not to want to buy in. And Miami is the only place where the Cuba they loved and taught me to love still exists. The way things are going on the island, that may never change, which only makes me love Miami that much more. But mostly, I like being here for exactly the same reason you would have heard from a lot of other people here: As a Cuban, I just feel at home in Miami in a way that I don't anywhere else in the world that I've lived in."

Moreno was an intellectual, an ebullient man whose interests—his academic specialty was Cuban-American politics—as much as his feelings must have played a role in his decision to settle in South Florida. He had reimmersed himself in his Cubanness willingly. But others, whose interests did not run either to Dade County electoral politics or to discussions of *el tema,* and, indeed, who had mixed feelings about living in the region at all, tended to share Moreno's sense that to live in Miami as a Cuban—it was always possible, of course, to live among non-Cubans, or in the fashionable, international world of Miami Beach's art deco district, whose mores had more in common with Lower Manhattan, or Berlin, or Santa Monica, California, than they did with the world of *el exilio*—was to participate in what was at once a radical simplification and an intensification of one's ethnic identity. Particularly for those who were touched by the belief, so endemic to the new multiculturalist ethic in America, that all identity was fixed, to return to Miami was to return not simply to a place, but to one's true self. In Miami, and, perhaps, only in Miami, it was possible to become Cuban, as the expression went, *en carne y hueso,* "in flesh and bone." And it went without saying that those who did not subscribe to the authority of these claims, and for whom the identity Miami proffered seemed like an imposition rather than a revelation of one's "true" self, felt as oppressed by Miami as people like Dario professed to feel liberated by it.

In the late fall of 1991, I met a young Cuban-American college student named Raul Martinez. He was engaged to be married to the non-Cuban daughter of one of Mitchell Kaplan's employees at Books and Books, and I got to know him because Mitchell had given him a temporary job helping out with the accounts receivable and the shipping and I was using the bookshop's office as a Miami base. Raul had been born in South Florida, but, like Dario Moreno, he had grown up in Southern California, in Huntington Beach, just south of L.A. He had only returned to Miami when he was about to enter high school, and he said he had never taken to it. Raul missed the West—America, as he once called it, in my hearing, an expression one might have expected to hear from a Dade County Anglo of fifty, not a Cuban-American of twenty— and, as if to advertise his determination to return there as soon after graduation as possible, he would frequently turn up for work wearing a T-shirt or a cap emblazoned with the logo of some Los Angeles–area sports team. One morning, as we were sitting in the Books and Books office and the phones, for once, were silent, Raul spelled out for me the gap that he saw between Miami and the rest of the country.

"It's two worlds," he explained, "two planets. Over in L.A., Mexicans try to learn English. I know people often don't give them credit for wanting to, but they try. Here in Miami, though, every Cuban makes a big point of speaking Spanish. The Federal Express guy who comes here, who probably speaks English himself, and, anyhow, knows he's delivering packages to an English-language bookstore, half the time will only talk to you in Spanish. *'Debes aprender,'* 'You must learn,' he said to Mitchell the other day. No wonder the people here go crazy. The guy's a Cuban. If he were a Nicaraguan, or a Costa Rican, he would try. But for

Cubans, it's almost like being outside, at work or wherever, is practically the same thing as being inside the house with your family. And it is like family living here. No matter where you go in Miami, everyone seems to know everyone else. I remember when I first went to high school and saw everyone kissing each other on the cheek the first day, I got completely freaked. I said to myself 'Hey, wait a second, are they all related or what?' And my family changed too. We hadn't talked about Cuba very much in California, even though my grandfather was a pretty well-known amateur boxer there and must have had a lot of memories. But I noticed that almost as soon as we all moved back to Florida, he started talking about Cuba more and more, as if once he got here he was really a whole lot happier living in the past.''

I later told this story to Raul Rodriguez, who, after nodding appreciatively, put it in a somewhat more general context. ''It's not so much that the guy's grandfather is getting lost in the past,'' he said, ''although I know that goes on all the time here in Miami. He's found another reality, one that in California of all places, where Cubans are probably more assimilated—not only less Cuban, but even less *Hispanic*—than anywhere else in the country, he had lost. For a guy to grow up in Cuba, and then live among sights and sounds that are totally foreign for years, and then return to a place where it's 'Varadero' this and 'la Habana' that and 'Pinar del Río' the other, is like going halfway back to Cuba. Maybe it's like a German refugee who came to the States fleeing Hitler going back to Switzerland or something; that's not exact, but you see what I mean. The real point is that when any of us leave Miami, even Ninon's parents, whom you've met and who couldn't be more Cuban, working in Chicago for all those years, we change. And though I know you think that we put too much store on Cuban identity as something fixed, you can't deny that it's not just 'professional Cubans' that become more Cuban when they come back here, it's all of us.''

The way in which this return to Cubanness might manifest itself varied according not simply to people's individual temperaments but also to their social class. Ninon Rodriguez's father, Frank Lavernia, who had gone to the University of Havana on a basketball scholarship, tended to remember striving middle-class men like himself, while Raul's mother, Esther Beltran, remembered the Havana nightlife and the upper-class party set of the fifties. Probably, Raul Martinez's grandfather remembered the smoky amphitheaters where the great fighters of the era, like Kid Chocolate, had done their wet work. Moreover, various social classes had various social institutions in the exile to represent their version of their lost country. Teresita de Blank could join the Sugar Growers' Association, but a factory worker from Hialeah might well be drawn to the Municipios de Cuba en el Exilio, an association of 114 of the 135 municipalities that had existed on the island before the revolution and that held regular elections to the councils and mayoralties of towns most of those doing the voting had not set eyes on for at least twenty years. And Raul Rodriguez, who belonged to American organizations like the South Florida Historical Society, and exile bodies like FACE, could nevertheless sit in his architect's office in Coral Gables staring at albums of Cuban design from the late fifties, the modernist buildings of Havana, some of which had been commissioned by his own family, whose allure had made him dream, even as a small boy in Miramar, of becoming an architect himself.

From a distance, it might have seemed reasonable to sum up what had taken place in the Cubans' Miami exile as what V. S. Naipaul once called "a defect of vision," in the sense, as Naipaul phrased it, that "when men cannot observe, they don't have ideas; they have obsessions." And it was true that because they had not, for the most part, been allowed to return to Cuba, and because those who had made such visits did so under a psychological duress that was bound to affect the sense they made of the experience, the exiles were bound to be drawn to a reduced, almost dreamlike sense of what their Cuban identity really consisted of. Indeed, that was why many who were willing to shoulder the political opprobrium they would face in Miami, and the physical and psychic risks they would run in Havana, were still reluctant to board one of Aruca's Haiti Trans Air flights. "I'm not expecting Disney World," a Cuban-American filmmaker named Jose Cardona once told the *Herald*'s Elinor Burkitt, as he tried to explain why he had never made the trip even though Cuba and the sense of being Cuban had come increasingly to dominate his thinking, "but maybe I'm afraid of being disillusioned." Having been forbidden the chance of seeing for himself for so long, the prospect of being able to find out was bound to be almost as frightening as continued unknowing.

By 1992, Cuban Miami was cornered. Any movement was bound to seem dangerous, for it threatened the hard-won identity that building Miami into a Cuban city and preserving the group cohesion of the exile had conferred upon a people otherwise bereft of victories. This was why it made such human sense for *el exilio* to commit itself to either knowing or unknowing. To fully take in the bad news about Cuba, to admit that the U.S. embargo was leading to real suffering among people who were, after all, the relatives of the Miami Cubans, was to undermine the political resolve that was all the more necessary in a post-Communist world where if Fidel Castro was not overthrown soon, a transformed geopolitics might lead future American administrations to seek an accommodation with a Havana that no longer constituted a threat to U.S. interests. At the same time, to allow the Cuban identity of Miami to be transformed was an even greater threat to the idea that Cubans in America were exiles, not immigrants. For as soon as Miami became a place rather than a halfway house, the exile would be over, whether or not Fidel Castro had fallen. That thought was unbearable, at least to the many who still dreamed of return. And even those who no longer believed the tyrant ever would be deposed shared this sense that the destinies of Havana and Miami were intertwined. "If only Castro would fall," the exile poet and critic Armando Alvarez-Bravo once told me with a sigh. "We could leave then." He paused, and then added with a smile, "I don't mean return to Cuba, just leave Miami."

In the meantime, many Cuban-Americans were digging in, emphasizing, as much to themselves, it often seemed, as to their non-Cuban interlocutors, Miami's uniqueness. This could take the form of anger, the fervent insistence that whatever "Americans" might want, Miami would remain Cuban. "Anglos hate us," Gloria Sanchez had told me during the same conversation in which she had evoked Martin Luther King as the engineer of nonassimilation, "because we are not like Mexicans or Puerto Ricans. We won't get down on our knees. We accept some of America but not everything. We weren't just peasants," she continued. "We love our culture and the Mariel boatlift brought more Cuban culture here. Look at Arturo Sandoval, the jazz trumpeter. He could whip Dizzy Gillespie's ass any day of the week." And, more calmly, but no less implacably, Maria Cristina Herrera, a Miami academic and Christian Democrat activist, told an interviewer that "[Miami's success] is primarily due to the impact of the Cuban thing. This is why we are very arrogant, and we share that with the natives on the island, including '*Comandante en Jefe.*' We are very arrogant, so we don't take any bullshit from anybody."

But however easy it was to run across examples of this sort of pugnacious, defiant rhetoric in Cuban Miami, however much someone like Herrera could insist that the transformation of the city was the problem of non-Cubans, "not mine," the subtext of all this talk was that Miami was the only thing the exile had left, and that it was bound and determined to hold on to it. People would routinely insist that their children were becoming more and more aware of their Cuban roots, even though all the surveys and demographic studies indicated skyrocketing rates of intermarriage between Cubans and non-Cubans and the steady adulteration of "authentic" Cubanity under the hammer blows of American consumer culture and the passage of time. But this sense of being Cuban was, of course, about being Cuban in Miami rather than being Cuban in Cuba. Gloria Sanchez insisting that Dade County should become a separate state, or Maria Cristina Herrera saying that she would speak Spanish wherever and whenever she pleased—this was an exaggeration; she was far too polite to do anything of the sort—was unlikely to have any effect on the political future of the island, only on the political future of South Florida, and even then, in an America that was becoming, thanks largely to immigration from Mexico, increasingly bilingual anyway, probably less than many Miamians, both Cuban and non-Cuban, imagined.

Older Cubans were preserving their Havana roots, but their

children, more often than not, were more concerned with redis-
covering their Miami ones. This doting Cuban parents would
describe proudly, as if the process demonstrated that the exile
was still alive and well. "My son didn't ever really think of
himself as being Cuban," Pedro Freyre once said to me, in
response to a question about assimilation among Cubans in their
teens and early twenties. "But when he went away to college at
Georgetown, that all changed. During his freshman year, I went
up to see him and to my astonishment all he wanted to do was talk
about Miami. I'll confess to you that I was delighted to hear him
talk in this way, but I also recognized that to his roommates he
must have been as monotonous in evoking the way Miami used
to be—and at one point he started to complain that Little Havana
wasn't Cuban anymore, that at the rate things were going in five
years it would be an Asian neighborhood—as I can be when I
start talking about Havana."

It would have been surprising if many young Cuban-Americans
had not felt that way. For thirty-three years, it had been drummed
into them that they were different, that the situation in South
Florida was unique, and that Cubanness was all but a genetic
characteristic. Like the Japanese, who will sometimes say in
private that those among them who speak a foreign language too
ably become, somehow, less authentically Japanese, the Miami
Cubans worried incessantly about the adulteration of their Cubanity, even as they insisted that such a catastrophe could never
take place. And accompanying this had been the psychological
hunkering down that has always been the hallmark of both the
political refugee and the immigrant, the sense that everything
outside the enclave is dangerous, and that one can only trust
family. In the case of Cuban Miami, this was consciously construed as meaning the extended family of *el exilio,* as much as
one's own blood relations. Only Cubans would understand,
whether the understanding in question was of one's cultural style
or, more profoundly, of one's pain—of the wound of exile.

What was less clear was whether the inculcation of this simultaneously homey and exalted sense of belonging could long survive the exiles' experience in the United States, particularly if

Fidel Castro did not fall soon. Although they were bound to loom larger in an age of multiculturalism and the quest for roots than they had in the America of enforced assimilation and the melting pot, American ethnic groups had never been untouched by the sorts of conceits that were displayed in such extreme form in Cuban Miami. American Jews had been like Miami Cubans a generation or two earlier. For someone familiar with both communities, there was a sense in which to travel around Cuban Miami was to find oneself surrounded by an improbable congeries of Spanish-accented Eddie Cantors, Philip Roths, and Saul Bellows. Only instead of going on about Jewish subjects, Jewish angst, Jewish disdain for the gentiles (what was Gloria Sanchez's remark about Sandoval, after all, but a Cuban version of this old American trope?), and, above all, Jewish particularity, the Cubans offered themselves. The constant talk of *el tema* was reminiscent of the old Jewish joke in which a Frenchman, an Englishman, and a Jew go to Africa. They each write books when they return home. The Frenchman's is called *The Love Life of the Elephant*; the Englishman's is called *The Migratory Patterns of Elephants*; and the Jew's is called *The Elephant and the Jewish Question*. It could just as well have been told about Cubans.

American Jews, too, had been as easily provoked into anger and clannishness by the perceived slights of outsiders as any Miami Cuban at her most extreme. When Gloria Sanchez, in the middle of her tirade, had mentioned in passing that, during their courtship, she had often asked the Puerto Rican doctor whom she would eventually marry whether he was "sure" he wasn't Cuban, it reminded me of nothing so much as the immigrant Jews who had liked to say that any intelligent gentile had a "Jewish head"—"*eine Yiddischer kopf*," as they used to say on the Lower East Side of New York as late as the nineteen-fifties. And yet in less than two generations, American Jews had gone from being the most insular of American ethnic groups to one whose sense of its own communal identity had been permanently fractured by intermarriage and assimilation. And although the parallel between Zionism and the Cuban dream of return was hardly exact—much as people like Jorge Mas Canosa liked to insist upon it—even Zionism had proved a far more transient vehicle than anyone might have predicted a generation before for imposing and fostering solidarity and identity. It was by no means clear, whatever people in Miami might hope and say, that if and when Castro fell there would not be many checkbook Cubans in Miami, just as, to use David Ben-Gurion's contemptuous description of the American Jews who had not moved to Israel but contributed to it financially, there were checkbook Zionists in the United States.

There were obvious differences, of course. The Cuban exile, even in the speeded-up twentieth century, had only lasted for a few decades. Cuba, unlike Israel, had existed within living memory, and was a hundred and forty miles away, not thousands. Most of all, Cuban Miami existed. There had been no Zionist Brooklyn in 1948, when the state of Israel had been proclaimed. But there were also ways in which Cuban Miami's attachment to its own identity, no matter how fierce and profound, depended too strongly on fairly small characteristics being invested with a weight and uniqueness that it was by no means clear they could bear for long. If Fidel Castro fell soon, that would be one thing. But if he lingered on, and the generation of exiles who had lived in Cuba as adults died, leaving only generations of people either born in the U.S. or raised there since childhood, would this Cubanity be more than another American quest for roots? The exile might well, in the long run, be defeated precisely by the strategy that had allowed it to maintain its coherence for three and half decades. For to have said that Cubanity was both ineffable, and, finally, a matter of attachment to things like food and music was finally to exclude too much of what middle-class people needed for their own sense of well-being. People might not need Virgilio Piñera, but they needed more than *palomilla* steaks, or the music of Arturo Sandoval.

As long as the dream of return, the belief in carrying on the struggle between the exile and the Castro regime, and the need to preserve Miami not only as a Cuban city but as a second, alternate Havana could be maintained, as long as Cuba could be kept alive in the heart of Miami, the exile could continue to believe in itself. But separation from Cuba was making it harder and harder to pass such beliefs from generation to generation. "Our sky, our earth, our spirit, that's Cuba," Luis Botifoll had once said to me, and, of course, he was in a position to know. But, by definition, members of the younger generation could only imagine. Even those completely committed to their belief in a Cuban identity recognized the fact. As Jose Cardona put it, "they say that being in exile is like dying a thousand deaths. But imagine being exiled from a country you've never seen." What he did not say, and certainly did not want to believe, was that feeling in exile from a country one had never seen was going to grow more and more difficult, no matter how often, in Cuban Miami, the sorrows and tribulations of individual lives, the tragedies and the everyday unhappiness, were added to the bill of exile.

There were, moreover, small indications that even on the level of food and music, in Cuban Miami the center was not holding, or, at least, was being altered far more rapidly than people cared to imagine. The Cuban music most people listened to was the Cuban-American sound of Gloria Estefan and the Miami Sound Machine, not Celia Cruz or Olga Guillot. And as Cubans had become more prosperous, fewer and fewer were willing to work in bastions of Cubanity like the Versailles and La Habana Vieja. People might repair to these places for their "fixes," as much cultural as culinary, of *ropa vieja,* or the pork sandwiches called *medianoches,* but it was increasingly likely that they would be served this soul food by a non-Cuban staff who had been completely ignorant of its existence before their own immigration to Miami from countries like Nicaragua, Panama, or Costa Rica. Indeed, it was becoming common to hear Cuban patrons in these restaurants calling exasperatedly for the (Cuban) maître d'hotel to complain about an order that the Central American waiter had managed to bungle. "It's a shock going there," wrote the Cuban-American critic Enrique Fernandez. "Those Cuban waitresses who called you *'mi amor'* and *'mi cielo'* have almost all disappeared."

The contrast between wished-for community and the synthetic realities of late-twentieth-century America could be even more arresting. One Saturday afternoon, the Rodriguezes and I decided to have lunch at one of Raul's favorite Cuban cafeterias in Coral Gables. As we entered the restaurant, Raul paused to peer at the photographs of Havana that, as was the case in so many of these places all over Greater Miami, graced the narrow corridor between the rear entrance in from the parking lot and the main dining room. "This one's a contemporary shot of the Malecón," Raul said excitedly. "Do you see that car there?" He pointed to a corner of the grainy image. "That's a Lada, a Russian Fiat. You remember, that's almost all we saw when we were in Havana."

In this atmosphere of reminiscence and Cubanity, we sat down, images of the Morro Castle, the Malecón, the Nacional Hotel, and other Havana landmarks surrounding us on all four walls. The people eating there that day were as Cuban as the photos, and Ninon even ran into a relative, just back from Chicago and eager for his first good Cuban meal in weeks. To all appearances, it was the prototypical Southwest Miami cafeteria. Hand-lettered signs advertised the day's specials and the big-bottomed waitresses— here, they were still Cubans—moved authoritatively, if somewhat perilously, between the tables on high-heeled shoes. But there was a change. It is rare to see black people in Cuban Miami anyway, so when a dark-skinned busboy came over to fill our glasses with ice water both the Rodriguezes and I were somewhat curious. Perhaps embarrassed by his attentiveness, Raul asked in Spanish for a basket of bread. But the man looked back blankly. A moment later, one of the waitresses came over and said, "Bread," distinctly and in English, and the man nodded and moved off toward the kitchen. Turning to Raul, she shrugged, and, reverting to Spanish, said, "They're all Haitians now."

Later that day, at Raul's office, we told the story to Tony Quiroga, who, like Raul, tended to work on Saturday afternoons. "There you are," Tony said. "We've become a successful American ethnic group, with foreigners working in our restaurants to prove it." Raul flinched, then shook his head and laughed. This was not the Miami of *el exilio,* nor was it a refuge from both Fidel Castro and the United States, but it was the Miami that was being born all around him, and Raul knew it. More importantly, he realized that it was this city, rather than the place of exile in which he had grown up, that his son would inhabit. And the discomfiting thought occurred to him, he told me later, that not only people but feelings were mortal, and that the exile, for all its bluster, which could be heard everywhere, might itself be entering its dotage.

8

THE POSSIBILITY THAT the real story of the Cuban exiles of South
Florida in the early nineties was of a community well on its way
to Americanization—though of the novel sort now in vogue in the
post-melting-pot United States—and that, as a group, it either
would have to get the chance to return to Cuba soon or, however
reluctantly, would have to accept the idea that even when return
did become an option (and it would; even the Castro regime's
defenders acknowledged that Communism would end with the
Maximum Leader) too few Miami Cubans would still want to
seize it, only seemed to inflame the passions of those who ached
to return and mute those who did not. The men and women who
loved their lost island, who lived and breathed *el tema,* were
horrified by the existence of a younger generation so far along in
their indifference to her that they were loath even to acknowledge
its existence. They comforted themselves with the idea that Cuba,
as a ruling passion, would again capture the hearts of their children and grandchildren when the opportunity for return presented
itself, no matter how engrossed at the moment young people in
Miami were by their careers and their American pleasures. As
long as people continued to feel Cuban, I was often told, albeit
somewhat defensively, then access to a sense of self that was not
simply "culturally" Cuban, by which people really meant Miamian or Cuban-American, but nationalistically Cuban had not
been barred for good. In the meantime, middle-aged and elderly
exiles took pride in their children's accomplishments, and, how-

ever unconsciously, encouraged every expression of Cuban particularity, or, even, on occasion, fostered it.

Younger Cubans often felt trapped between the manners of their parents and the styles they were attracted to as middle-class American kids. An advertising executive in Miami named Tere Zubizarreta, who had been the first Cuban-American named to the Orange Bowl Committee—a high honor in boosterist, sports-mad South Florida—told me proudly of an argument she had overheard between her son and her daughter. The girl had been speaking loudly, Tere said, and "my son asked her to tone it down. But my daughter turned on him and asked, 'Why shouldn't I shout? Aren't I Cuban?' And I thought, 'Good for her. She should be proud of who she is.' "

But, of course, who Tere Zubizarreta's daughter "was" could not, however much some Cuban exiles might wish to insist on the point, be described as a fixed category. For all the multiculturalist talk, and, more importantly, for all the investment people in *el exilio* were bound to have in an essentialist conception of identity, even the older generations behaved differently from the way they had twenty years before. The Cuban Miami David Rosemond had described, with its chaperones, its high rate of church attendance, and an economic life that largely took place within the enclave, had opened up by the mid-eighties. In trendy nightclubs on Miami's South Beach and malls in suburban Kendall, there was very little difference, in appearance, in accent, or in casual conversation, between young, middle-class Cuban Miamians and their non-Cuban peers. In a country less obsessed with distinctions based on race or ethnicity and more alive to solidarities based on class, there would have been nothing surprising about such an observation. But in the United States in the early nineties all the attention was focused on either the seemingly inescapable identities based on skin pigment or accent or the elective identities of preference, sexual and otherwise. And if, for these reasons, most Americans were having an increasingly difficult time perceiving their similarities, the problem was far more acute for Cuban Miamians who either were intent on maintaining at least the possibility of difference or had grown up believing in its fundamental relevance to their own lives.

An outsider might find some of the common definitions of what made a Cuban different from a non-Cuban to be, leaving the question of exile itself to the side, something of an anticlimax. After all the drama, what did Cubanness consist of? When Manning Salazar, a Cuban-American filmmaker who had grown up in Brazil, told the *Herald*'s Elinor Burkitt about his trip to the island aboard one of Aruca's flights, and of how his weeklong stay had reinforced his sense of his own Cuban identity, the elements that made up this sense of self were largely stylistic. "Mostly what I learned," he reported, "was how Cuban I was—in my family relations, the way I move my hands, my tendency to yell, my informality and hospitality." Were these really qualities that set Cubans apart from American Jews, or Italians, or Puerto Ricans? It hardly seemed likely. More revealing was Manning's admission that he had never felt Cuban, even in Miami, whereas in Havana he "looked around and saw a whole island full of Cubans; the policeman, the bus driver, everyone was Cuban. Everyone was like me."

That confident "was," again. There were eleven million people in Cuba. They come, as people in every country do, in all sorts of versions. Indeed, outside of official government propaganda, it is generally not the case that people on the island talk about a monolithic Cuban identity or a single, defining Cuban characterology, the way people so often do in Miami. In this sense, as in so many others, the exile had preserved an enhanced Cubanness, one that had perhaps obtained in the nineteen-forties and fifties but that had withered under Communism and probably would have been weakened even if Fidel Castro had never come to power. It was that islander's sense of separateness, combined with an immigrant's enthusiasm for his or her adopted country. The great immigration to Cuba from Spain had taken place in the early part of the twentieth century. That was when the villages of Galicia, Asturias, and Catalonia had been emptied as people headed by the tens of thousands for a better life in Matanzas or Pinar del Río, just as in the hundreds of thousands the poor of

Sicily and the Russian Pale had headed for New York. In the Asturian Pavilion at Expo '92 in Seville, there was even a panorama of this emigration—"indianos," "Indians," was the way those who remained in Spain described those who made the crossing—with a steamer trunk on which the words had been chalked, "Gone to Camagüey."

The first generation of immigrants had been Spaniards, pure and simple. Those who had prospered had erected great *beauxarts* piles in the center of Havana—the Galician Club, the Asturian Club, and the Catalan Club—and, along with the capitol building, the presidential palace, and the Spanish embassy, these had dominated the city's skyline until the great post–World War II building boom had created a Miami Beach–style high-rise corridor along the far end of the Malecón. But the Spaniards' children had been Cubans, and their nationalism had had the particular fervor of grateful immigrants. Another generation or two, and, like their Jewish and Italian opposite numbers in the United States, they might have learned to wear the motley of their patriotism more lightly. But they never had the chance. Fidel Castro came down from the Sierra Maestra in triumph; they went into exile in Miami; and attitudes that otherwise would almost certainly have altered under the pressures of time and history— imagine anything remaining static in any bourgeois world, particularly one as sophisticated as the Cuban during the nineteen-sixties—were, like memories of golden childhoods unrevised by adult pleasures and rewritings, left frozen in place.

Only in the hothouse atmosphere of Miami could the patriotism of the exile, which was, in fact, the patriotism of the Cuban bourgeoisie, circa 1959, the idealization of place, which was, for its part, the idyllic sense of security of a privileged childhood, and the simplified sense of what identity consisted of, which was the price and privilege of Miami's beleaguerment, have joined together to produce this modern-day version of the Fall that was all but the official ideology of *el exilio*. Nostalgia, lyricism, and loss had done their work. "Mienteme," "Lie to Me," was the title of an Olga Guillot song popular just before Fidel Castro had entered Havana. The Cuban bourgeoisie had sung it then, and, for all its success in South Florida, was still singing it. Now its message was "Tell me I will still return home to Cuba," "Tell me the exile is not permanent," and, most touchingly of all, "Tell me this adulthood, this *American* adulthood, is not the only destiny that remains." And if the lie was harder and harder to maintain, not because Fidel Castro would not eventually fall, but because he would, in all likelihood, leave power too late, there were many in Cuban Miami, young as well as old, who seemed to be singing all the louder to drown out the bad news, in the hope of preserving their Cubanness in the interstices of their American lives.

It was the confluence of having identified themselves for so long—quite justifiably—as exiles and the American rediscovery of ethnic identity that made the Cubanness of Miami seem more solid than it really was in the early nineties. When people could say they were exiles, not immigrants, and, when pressed, fall back on the assertion that they felt "culturally" Cuban, it was easy to get the impression that there was one Cuban Miami. But, in reality, the sense of being foreigners stuck in an alien environment and the sense of wanting to carve out yet another special corner in a balkanized America were anything but the same thing. And a new generation was coming into adulthood whose *parents* had grown up in South Florida. It was the Calle Ocho that Pedro Freyre's son was nostalgic for, specifically for a Calle Ocho without Central Americans, not, like his father, the Malecón or Varadero Beach. If Manning Salazar was entranced, during his visit to Havana, by the fact that everyone he met was Cuban, this had as much if not more to do with the polyglot nature of life even in Miami, and the fact that ethnic homogeneity is now restricted to either the poorest or the most Communist of countries, than anything else. Whether he knew it not, the Cuba he visited was in a time warp as much because of this lack of non-Cubans—had Castro not won and, as so many Miami Cubans suggested, the island become more and more prosperous, one effect would have surely been massive emigration from other, less favored parts of the Caribbean, as Venezuela had experienced during the same period, not to mention Miami—as because of its collapsing "command" economy. And even Salazar, for all his enthusiasm, admitted sorrowfully that things were changing in Miami, that "people here are losing the sense of what it means to be Cuban."

More often than not, this was taking place quietly. Defections from *el exilio* were only rarely put into words, though obviously declarations of fidelity to it tended to be eloquent and ostentatious. Indeed, both those who still cared and those who, if they had been called upon to voice their sentiments, might well have regretfully concluded that though they wished Cuba well they had no intention of returning or even involving themselves in the island's post-Castro destiny seemed to prefer to keep the matter of Americanization tacit. Non-Cuban Miamians, locked in their demonizing view of the exile, might attribute this reluctance to some putative fear of sanction, a Mafialike code of silence that caused Cuban Miamians of all persuasions on the matter to present a solid front to outsiders, much as they might bicker among themselves. The reality, however, was less melodramatic, and, in most cases anyway, had more to do with people's affection for one another—Cubans might bicker, and, where politics was concerned, become odious and even occasionally violent, but family piety generally outweighed politics, any politics—than with the fact that they were afraid their careers might suffer if they said the wrong thing, let alone that they might be harmed physically.

To state unequivocally not only that return definitively no longer figured in one's plans, but also that one had largely succeeded in banishing the prospect from one's dreams as well, was, in the world of *el exilio,* practically the same thing as saying that one rejected the world in which one had grown up and the family members, actual and extended, who had peopled that world. Certainly, such declarations would make harmony at family get-togethers all but impossible to maintain. In almost every family in Cuban Miami, there was bound to be an Uncle Pepe or an Aunt Thelma for whom Cuba remained the cause. And that Pepe was the doting relative who had taken you to watch the Yankees at their spring training camp in Fort Lauderdale, that Thelma the consoling presence who saw you through your first broken heart. To repay their devotion by causing them such pain, when all you had to do was keep your own counsel, made no human sense at all. Far better to get on with your American life in Westchester, or Coral Gables, or Kendall, while paying lip service, every now and again, to the pieties of exile. And after all, though the cultural differences between Cubans and non-Cubans were frequently exaggerated, the overwhelmingly Catholic Cubans had never been particularly persuaded by the post-Protestant American middle-class notion that it was important to say everything you felt and thought, no matter how much pain such expressions caused those you cared for.

This Catholic human maturity—the quality northern European Protestants have usually confused with cynicism—made demands on those who still believed in *la causa* as well. A Tere Zubizarreta might beam when her daughter insisted on her Cubanity, but though she might insist that she cried whenever her plane crossed over Cuban airspace, which was only a melodramatic formulation of the love for Cuba that was the bedrock of the exile's cohesion, she hardly expected tears to well up in her children's eyes. It was enough that they did not tell her that she was weeping for no reason, that she had better things to do, on a business flight from Miami to Caracas, than mourn a country she had left when she was a little girl.

Tere's children were grown. In families with younger kids still living at home, the outlines of the bargain that had been struck between the adults who spoke of Cuba and the children who watched Miami Heat games were even clearer. Raul Rodriguez's office was decorated with images of Havana and of his work. In Raul and Ninon's bedroom at home, there were portraits of the family on the dresser and a stack of books on Cuba by the bed ranging from standard works like Hugh Thomas's history of the island to books on Miami by Joan Didion and myself in which the Rodriguezes had figured. But in Ruly's room, there were only the icons of an American twelve-year-old from a prosperous family: posters of sports stars—the basketball player Michael Jordan caught in mid-leap, an old-timey image of Lou Gehrig of the

1920s-era New York Yankees—as well as a basic Apple computer, a poster reading, "I like my room this way," and a Nintendo system. In the evenings, at the dinner parties that Ninon Rodriguez gave with such indefatigable generosity, the conversation might be about Cuba. By 1992, the Rodriguezes were well enough known on the island, and among experts on Cuba in Washington and New York as well, that it was a rare visitor from any of these worlds who did not make his or her way to the house off Sunset Drive at some point during a stopover in Miami. But if the conversations in the living room were so often in Spanish and about Cuba, it was possible, in moments when the talk died down, to hear the blare of the television broadcasting a ball game from Ruly's room, to hear the boy talking, in English naturally, with his friends, or to have him come running out to announce to Raul, "Dad, the Yankees just scored two runs," or "Dad, you should have seen the catch Canseco just made!"

At those moments, Raul would shake himself out of the exile mind-set from which he had been operating, put aside the questions over which he had been arguing with his wife and his guests—Would the Cuban government's attempt to create a tourist sector succeed? What were the implications of the Torricelli bill? And, always, what would be Cuba's fate?—and become again, for a time, a doting Cuban-American father. He might insist, over Ruly's objections, that the boy make the trips to Cuba, but at home in Miami Raul watched his son grow up American and, those visits aside, made no attempt to arrest the process. It was as if the bilingualism that was so much the rule in Cuban Miami, both in business and in private life, had an analogue in a kind of psychological bilingualism of family relations. These alternating currents were not always easy to regulate—Teresita de Blank had admitted to me that her children resented the amount of time she spent at Sugar Growers meetings: "A meal with them is a meal missed with my kids," she'd said—and obviously, there were moments when, on both sides of the generational and affective divides, people chafed at having to keep their real feelings to themselves, but what was remarkable in the end about Cuban Miami was how hard all the exile generations seemed to be trying not to provoke each other with blatant expressions of disagreement.

Part of the way in which this subtle, difficult harmony was maintained was by what seemed to be a tacit agreement that those who were still faithful to Cuba would do most of the talking, especially in public, and, in return, they would not inquire too closely into what those who had strayed were actually doing with their lives. It was interesting that the people who were criticized in Cuban Miami were those who *asserted* their claim not to feel Cuban (those who supported Castro, like Andres Gomez of the Antonio Maceo Brigades, were also stigmatized, but they were a tiny group in South Florida) rather than those who simply personified it. And the fact that Cuban-Americans who had no interest in the island in terms of their own individual futures at least paid lip service, and often were genuinely captivated by the idea of Cubanness as a matter of roots, meant that even if the more vertical members of *el exilio* had wanted to exact a higher level of devotion it would have been all but impossible for them to have done so. One of the advantages of the new American ideal of "diversity" was that it implied that one had to give up nothing of one's linguistic and ethnic past while, of course, all the while what was really taking place was an erosion of that past in all but its most totemic, incantatory form. To say, "I feel Cuban," or "I'm comfortable with my Cuban roots," was enough. Like a pagan paying lip service to the gods of conquering Rome by erecting a little niche to Jupiter in the corner of a temple of Baal or Isis, Cuban-Americans who had moved on were only required not to say so. As far as everything else was concerned, they could more or less do as they liked.

Time and again in Cuban Miami, I would spend an evening in which the conversation was dominated by people who insisted that the exile was intact, or boasted that Cubans were a special case in America—that they were different and always would be different—or, most commonly of all, that nothing could be decided about the situation of *every* Cuban-American until Castro was removed from power and people were free to choose who they wanted to be (this notion of selecting one's identity, made in the name of enduring Cubanity, in fact demonstrated just how Americanized the exiles had become, for who apart from Americans thinks these matters a question of choice?), only to discover that the real dynamics of the people at the dinner table were rather more complicated than such pronouncements made them appear. Unless one found oneself in the heart of the political exile itself, among officials of the Foundation, say, or at one of Maria Cristina Herrera's famous *tertulias* (the Spanish term connoted a gathering halfway between a salon and a cell meeting), where only the professionally committed, the devout of *el exilio,* were likely to be found, there were almost invariably people in attendance whose own ways of living belied the monolithic images being propounded by those doing the talking. When, for example, Gloria Sanchez had insisted, on the rancorous night I spent with her, that "my father told me what Miami was like before we came; it was a big zero," and, having established to her own satisfaction the exile's claim to having built the city up, went on to insist brassily that "we Cubans have the right to make the rules here," it was not that anyone else in attendance argued with her but that, by what they said about their own lives and ambitions, it was plain that their feelings were quite different.

It was not simply that several younger Cuban-Americans bridled visibly when Gloria, perhaps carried away by her own rhetoric, insisted that Spanish might eventually supplant English in Dade County, although, since their own Spanish was getting rusty, they were anything but delighted by the prospect. Those who remained impassive were more interesting still. One of these last was a man named Andres Rivero. He was in his mid-thirties, with long limbs and the studied calm that hints at money and class assurance. It turned out that his grandfather had been Fulgencio Batista's last prime minister. Rivero, of course, had left Havana as a small child. Now, he worked in the U.S. attorney's office for the Southern District of Florida, where, Raul Rodriguez told me later, he had already made a name for himself as a man with a big career before him.

Early in the evening, I asked him what it was like to carry the baggage of his family's political history in Miami. "It's important in the family context,'' he replied, after a pause. ''I care about my family, about what they went through. But, you see, I'm making my life here now. It's a question of making the right distinctions.''

He said little more. For the rest of the time we spent together, he sat quietly, sometimes smiling gently, and often clasping the hand of his American wife, who looked in the third trimester of her pregnancy. Gloria Sanchez's voice rose and fell. Around seven thirty, Rivero rose, and, after thanking his hosts, said with an apologetic shrug, ''Well, this has been fun, but we've got to get going. We've got tickets for the Heat game tonight, and you know how bad the traffic gets around the Omni.'' And then, after shaking hands with me, and embracing our hosts, a colleague from the U.S. attorney's office named Lauren Priegues and her handsome husband, Lazaro, a young Cuban-American doctor, Rivero and his wife were gone—literally, from the poolside table behind the Priegueses' little Coral Gables bungalow, and, I thought, metaphorically, from *el tema,* as well.

Later, though, it struck me that at no point in the evening had Rivero voiced the slightest disagreement with Gloria Sanchez and, to a lesser extent, Lazaro Priegues, who had made some of the same points less stridently—''Miami is the only place in America where we Cubans can be ourselves,'' he'd said; ''everywhere else we're condescended to as 'Hispanics.' '' Nonetheless, though he belonged to the most vertical of families, the center of gravity had obviously shifted for him. Rivero worked for the U.S. government; he had married outside the exile, as so many Miami Cubans were doing; in short, he had simply moved on. In this, he reminded me of Raul Rodriguez's brother Frank, also a lawyer, also married to an American woman, also most of the way out of *el exilio* and into the American mainstream. Frank would have cheerfully admitted that he had a different and a more difficult past than most of his non-Cuban colleagues in the Florida Bar Association, but he would have been incredulous had it been proposed to him that he had a different *future* from any of them. Nor, interestingly, did his older brother, Raul, ever suggest the point; he was as tactful with his brother as he was with his son.

For all the shouting that accompanied political discussions in Cuban Miami, it was, in fact, a community in which so many people, at great cost to themselves, given how strongly they felt, were desperately trying to be tactful. Andres had not attacked Gloria, nor had Gloria challenged Andres. Raul and his brother groped for common ground. And Ruly Rodriguez cheered for Michael Jordan and the Chicago Bulls and, with more grace than could reasonably have been expected of him, without fanfare put up with the fact that too often discussions of *el tema* ruled the family dinner table.

But this tact could not entirely conceal the reality that in the careers of countless younger Cuban-American professionals like Frank Rodriguez and Andres Rivero, as much as in the appearance of Haitian busboys and Nicaraguan and Costa Rican waitresses in the cafeterias of Little Havana, the cocoon of Cubanity was fissuring. Even Gloria Sanchez was not immune. At a certain point, she complained that Cuban men in Miami were taking more docile Central American women for mistresses. "Doormats," she called them, adding that she had told her husband that she would shoot him "with a bow and arrow" if she ever caught him in bed with one. And yet, even in this little flourish of a story, Americanization loomed. In *la Cuba de ayer,* well-born girls had not talked, or thought, that way. As Teresita de Blank had said, they had grown up resigned to the idea that their husbands would be unfaithful to them. It was only in the eighties, in, precisely, Gloria Sanchez's generation, that the experience of America had emboldened Cuban-American women to think differently, to demand as well as to accept. If, as Manning Salazar had complained, "people here are losing the sense of what it means to be Cuban," they were losing these shackles of custom as well as their passion for the island.

There was indeed a sense in which, by the early nineties, Cubans in Miami were making the rules, just as Gloria Sanchez had boasted. But for *el exilio,* as opposed to for the Cuban ethnic enclave of South Florida, this situation was beginning to look more like a threat than a triumph. If Cubans were in a position to make the rules, it meant that, however much they might deny it, they were increasingly feeling at home. And the paradox was that the more comfortable they felt, the more the wound of exile would be stanched, and the more their defining pain went away, the less they would be able to consider themselves to be exiles. Their failure—the loss of Cuba—had led to success in Miami. Now that success was bringing failure for the exile in its train. Some people might rail against this, and insist that for them Cuban culture, their own identity, was everything. "I'm not interested in cable television, in cars, jewelry, and a nice house," a young filmmaker named Jose Cardona told Elinor Burkitt. "I'm into family, history, culture." But the problem was that the exile had, historically, been as insistent on achieving material success in Miami as on preserving the memory of Cuba. Now, as Cardona realized correctly, it was becoming apparent that there was a deep contradiction between these two ambitions.

For all the talk that the success of Cuban Miami had been based on ethnic solidarity, on Cubans doing business with other Cubans, and on establishing in Dade County a base of both economic and political power, by the nineties the limits of this approach were becoming clear. With the collapse of the savings and loan industry a few years earlier, the period when enterprising Cuban businessmen with relatively small amounts of capital could found banks ended definitively. The same pattern could be found in other businesses, like insurance and manufacturing, as well. If the exile community was to continue to be successful, it could not continue to be insular. And yet if it stopped being insular, then it would cease to be an exile community, at least in the way that it had been since 1959. Belatedly, perhaps, the bill for Cuban success in the United States as much as for the exile's failure to unseat Fidel Castro was being presented to the Miami community. And the fact that people did not know how they should pay, whether they should abandon the dream of return or, perhaps, distance themselves from the United States, did not mean that the reckoning could be postponed much longer. The hysteria of Cuban Miami in the early nineties was based on this as much as on the more visible emotional roller-coaster ride concerning Castro's fall on which it had been embarked since the collapse of the Soviet empire.

What idealistic young people like Jose Cardona were offering would have been unlikely to draw many adherents anywhere in the world, let alone in as mercantile a culture as that of Cuban Miami. Not for nothing did the exiles call themselves, and with great pride, "the Jews of the Caribbean," and brag of their business acumen. And if there was any point to being successful in business, it was precisely so that one could acquire all those consumer durables Cardona had decried—a car, fine jewelry, a nice house. To have turned their backs on such things, moreover, would have symbolized for the striving middle class of Cuban Miami turning their backs on everything they had accomplished, everything their shiny cars and beautiful homes proved they had accomplished. Moreover, whether Cardona realized it or not, to invite a businessman from Coral Gables—which was to say, someone who was probably the son and grandson of businessmen from Miramar or El Vedado—to accept the idea that what he had accumulated was less important than family, history, or culture was, among other things, to misunderstand the history of the Cuban middle class *before* it left the island. After all, the deep "culture" of the prerevolutionary Cuban bourgeoisie had been that of trade. Only from the vantage point of exile, or else from the naive perspective of childhood—children don't know how the things they acquire or the places in which they live are paid for, and there was a sense in which, with the distortions that time and yearning had wrought, many exiles cast the pleasures of their Cuban youths in the same terms—could it have appeared to be anything else. Benny Moré had not "been" Cuba. He had been a brilliantly talented performer who had entertained the people in whose hands the destiny of Cuba resided. It was pure sentimentality to pretend otherwise.

And yet to a large degree the exile had drawn its strength precisely from its residence in an imaginative world of pure feeling. The problem arose when people either seriously contemplated the prospect of return or, like Cardona, regretted the movement away from Cubanity among their peers, the children of the Miami exiles. People were not going to give up their comforts in the name of national feeling or a shared sense of Cubanness, particularly when the patriotism, that communal ardor, had, over time, become more and more grounded in emotional, extramaterial attachments to the island, a nub of shared tastes and gestures that all but ignored the material life. If they were to contemplate return seriously, then the emotional and the material had to be recoupled. And although the dominant view in Miami was that a return to the island, even for those exile businessmen who had no interest in living there, would be an extraordinary commercial opportunity, there were others who argued that the practical realities of life in Miami suggested a very different outcome.

Had the only people making such a demoralizing suggestion been either non-Cuban or members of younger, more Americanized cohorts of Cuban-Americans, it might have been possible to dismiss it. Indeed, if the case for Cuban Miami being more attached to Miami than to Havana had been made only with words, then other, more vertical spokespeople could probably have overwhelmed these hopeless predictions with their own implacable message that Cubans would always be prepared to return to their island, no matter how many more years they had to wait. But in the summer of 1992, nature itself seemed to collude with the doomsayers. In late August, the worst hurricane to strike the southeastern United States since the great hurricane of 1926 that had destroyed a large part of Miami came ashore, its epicenter in south Dade County around the city of Homestead. The devastation was incalculable, although compared to what people further south had experienced the prosperous areas of Cuban Miami escaped relatively lightly. Still, the beautiful live oaks and poincianas that so many exile householders had tended with such care, the tropical ferns, the creepers, and the palmettoes, were uprooted and destroyed. Raul Rodriguez only lost his garden. His partner, Tony Quiroga, lost his house.

One week later, the Rodriguezes, along with two hundred thousand of their neighbors, were still without air-conditioning or water. "We're flushing our toilet with the water from the neighbor's pool," Raul told me on the phone; the roads were still impassable, with volunteers standing in for the grid of traffic lights in the boiling heat of South Florida in August. Years before, Raul couldn't really remember exactly when, he had taken the screens off the windows. "We always use the air conditioner," he said. "Who thought there would be anything like Hurricane Andrew?" And as a result, he, Ninon, and Ruly had the choice of sweltering with the windows closed or being eaten alive by insects at night if they left the windows open. "We have been well bitten," Raul said shortly, and, after a pause, added, "I don't really care about that, but what kills me is losing the garden. Poincianas are incredibly fragile, you know."

As tragedies go, none of this signified a great deal. Raul himself was the first to insist on the point. But what the hurricane brought home, at least obliquely, was the degree to which Miami Cubans had taken the comforts of South Florida for granted. They had been so occupied imaginatively dreaming of the enchanted garden that Havana had been for them that they had lost sight of the real gardens in which they lived in Coral Gables, Westchester, and South Miami. The dream of return was a wish nurtured in comfort. The minute that comfort was taken away, the fragility of the present hove into view, at least temporarily blotting out both the past the exiles mourned and the future they had craved for so long. And so the full scope of the disaster began to sink in, and as Cuban-American families began to add up their losses, the easy talk of returning "home" to Cuba was stilled for a time—though in due course its full volume was restored, just like the air conditioners and plumbing of Cuban Miami—and people looked around their ruined front yards and realized that, in exile too, there was plenty to lose.

Not that they hadn't been warned, and by people committed to *el tema* as well as by those, more easily dismissible, who believed that it was time to let go of the dream. One of the most surprising of these skeptics was Miguel Tudela, one of the leaders of the Municipios. On the face of things, one would not have expected someone who had once led an organization whose principal goal had been to maintain a shadow administration of the municipalities of Cuba to question whether the Miami exiles really would return, even if given the chance, but Tudela, a spare figure in his late fifties, who made his living in Miami selling insurance, was hardly the fanatical exile that outsiders painted all members of the Municipios to be. To the contrary, he was far more realistic about the ways in which Cuba had changed since 1960, when, at twenty-six the youngest elected mayor on the island, he had been forced into exile. "People are always saying here in Miami that we are one people divided by a single man, Fidel Castro," he told me. "But that's not exactly right. Cuba is a different country from the one we left, with different social habits."

This might have been common sense in other parts of the world, but it was something most people in Miami thought twice before saying, particularly if, like Tudela, they believed that the changes were irreversible, whatever government took charge of the island. The more conventional expectation was the one voiced to me by the shadow warrior himself, Felix Rodriguez, who insisted that "the Cuban people have not changed that much. And since the Cuban people need the economic power of the exile, it will be a learning experience for them, both in terms of democracy and in terms of the free market. It's not so hard to go from a bad life to a good one. That will be a tremendous thing for the Cuban people to have happen to them."

What Rodriguez did not explain was why the Cuban people in Miami would necessarily want to go from their good life in South Florida to what, even in the rosiest of scenarios, would be a far more impoverished one in Havana or Santiago. This most specific of men when he was talking about campaigns he had waged or political intrigues he had participated in or witnessed could only produce the familiar emotional rationale for why the exiles and those that had remained would rebuild the island that had been the stock-in-trade of Cuban Miami for two generations. We had spoken in his trophy room. A rifle and mobiles of helicopters he had flown in Southeast Asia and Central America hung from the ceiling over the bar. On one wall there was a banner with three horizontal red stripes on a yellow background—the flag of the Republic of South Vietnam—and on another a Vietcong flag Rodriguez said he had captured himself. A U.S. flag stood on a medal stand, and, behind it, testimonials, medal citations, and presentation pistols hung from frames on the wall, as crowded together as paintings in an eighteenth-century portrait gallery. In another corner, there was a poster of the book jacket of his memoir, *Shadow Warrior,* with a typed legend underneath that read, "Recommended." And, of course, there was the blowup of the famous photo of Rodriguez standing next to Che Guevara just before the guerrilla leader was taken away and shot.

"I'm eager to go back to my country," he said. "Mentally, I know it's a different place—I've thought about return for so many, many years, and I recognize that what will happen can't be predicted. But what I do know is that we Cubans face a unique situation. In the exile, none of us lost the desire for the homeland because we had so many good memories. The problem is that there are so many people on the island who don't share them. I don't want them to migrate north to Florida. I want them to stay in Cuba and for all of us to rebuild the island together. That's what I've been fighting for during the past thirty years, and, now that we've finally won, I don't believe we aren't going to be successful. We had such a beautiful island, you know. There were so few of us who ever wanted to migrate—I know I never would have left—and we were blessed with so much . . . until Castro came in."

And perhaps, for Rodriguez, Miami really had been a way station in which he had spent half a lifetime. But his were exactly the kind of comments that Miguel Tudela had had in mind when he spoke of the exile's refusal to face facts about Cuba. "There's no Christmas in Cuba anymore," Rodriguez had said, his horror utterly genuine. "That will have to reestablished." Then, the soldier's practicality taking over, he added, "I suppose the first year we'll have to bring the Christmas dinners to Havana from Miami."

Unwilling to accept the idea that the changes in Cuba had gone too far to be changed by investment, charity, and fellow feeling, Rodriguez gave no sign, during the time I spent with him, of worrying whether Miami had changed out of all recognition as well. And yet though he was eager to return, he frankly admitted that neither his daughter, who lived in Europe, nor his son, who lived in Miami, were likely to go back to Cuba immediately. Indeed, he even mused at one point that perhaps the best solution would be to commute between Miami and Havana. "No one can look down on you in your own country," Rodriguez said at the end of our talk, as if that sealed the matter.

When I repeated this to Tudela, without identifying Rodriguez, he only smiled grimly. "I know half the people you speak to here say that they are going back," he said. "But think about it for a minute. They have lives, they're in school, or else they're starting up careers and families. Whenever I hear this kind of talk, I ask the person indulging in it, 'How old are you? Do you need to visit the doctor often, and, if you moved back to Cuba, would your health hold up?' Or else I ask, 'How is your business doing? Is it really solvent enough for you to pick up and move back to the island? How many kids do you have, and how many nieces and nephews? Do you have an aged parent depending on you for support? How much money have you put away? Is your mortgage paid? The car? Your children's college tuition? Next year's professional insurance?'

"What people hope for is not what is going to happen," he continued, "and the truth is that people here in Miami know it. Let me give you an example. As a businessman I have to say that if I heard an employee telling me, as people are always saying when *El Nuevo Herald* does its surveys, that the minute Cuba was free he was going to return there, I'd have to fire him on the spot. I might like to behave differently, but whatever I've done with the Municipios, when I'm at the office I'm running my business, not any crusade. And each employee I have represents an investment in time and training. If he's not going to stick around, the only responsible thing for me to do is to get rid of him and hire someone who will. Of course, the reason most employers don't behave in the way that I've described is that they know perfectly well that they're not going back and their employees are not going back. It's a wish, you see, not an intention."

If anything, Tudela understated what was going on. For the intention to return was being communicated with more and more difficulty across the generational divide. As the years went by,

Castro continued *not* to fall and the toll of discreet defections from within the exile itself continued to mount. No sector, no economic class, except, and even there to a lessening extent, among the people who had come to Miami after Mariel, was without its losses. A Luis Botifoll would have returned in a moment, had the opportunity presented itself. But his daughter Luisa, an architect who worked in Raul Rodriguez's firm, had made her life in Cuban Miami. Moreover, Luisa had a three-year-old daughter, and it was a foregone conclusion that unless things changed on the island very soon, that American daughter growing up in Luisa and her husband's sumptuous house in Coral Gables would be reason enough for her parents to remain where they were. Even Ruly Rodriguez, who, after all, had actually been on four trips to Cuba with his parents, could appear like a living rebuttal to the argument that Cuban-Americans would return.

One night, over dinner in South Miami, Ruly suddenly interrupted his parents' conversation with an account of a classmate, the son of a German businessman, who had given a report in class that day about Cuba. Raul appeared startled for a moment, and then, collecting himself, remarked quietly, "You should have done it, Ruly; after all, you've been there a lot."

"No," the boy replied emphatically, but, when his parents pressed him for a reason, he at first refused to say anything more than that he didn't want the attention. "You wouldn't mind if it were baseball," his father said. "I mean, you wouldn't intentionally strike out just so as not to stand out as a good player."

"Of course not," Ruly said, snorting. "But it's not the same. In school, all the teachers single you out. When I gave a presentation on Cuba at my last school"—he was studying in a special Spanish-English bilingual program that used many of the same textbooks as those one would find in a Madrid primary school—"they brought the Spanish consul general to hear me." He reddened, and then, lapsing into Spanish, he mimicked the teacher's words: " 'This is Raulito Rodriguez, he's been to Havana and knows all about Cuba.' "

Affectionately, but with his mounting frustration audible in his voice, Raul tried to press his son further. This only made Ruly more upset. "You see," he exclaimed finally, "it's not like baseball. There's no . . ." He fumbled for the word.

"You mean comparison," his father said.

"Yeah, comparison. Look, it's happening now. You keep talking about it on and on. You won't stop. Cuba. Cuba. Cuba."

He fell silent and turned away, staring out the window into the half-filled parking lot. Raul, Ninon, and I exchanged a glance, then began to talk rapidly—about architecture, about New York, about Miami-Dade Community College; about anything, that is, except *el tema*. A few minutes later, though, Ruly turned back toward us, and, in a calm voice, observed "You know, I have to say I say different things to different people about what my impressions of Cuba really were."

"You mean your grandmother," Raul said with a groan.

"Yeah," Ruly said.

"What about your classmates?" I asked.

"No, they don't care," the boy replied. And his mother added, "His little friends just talk about Nintendo and sports, right, Ruly?"

And this time, when he said "Yeah" one more time, it was with the relief of someone who had arrived at the heart of the matter. I could feel the exile vanishing before me.

9

Because the end of a great hope rarely comes in one single, easily delineable moment, and because even the bitterest of revelations often engender, among those forced to confront them, a renewed determination to remain faithful to the feeling that has been betrayed or the cause that has been lost, it was not surprising that in Miami, in 1992, people were simultaneously registering the disappointment they felt over the fact that Fidel Castro had not yet fallen and clinging to the belief that their return was still imminent, Cuba's future still bright. True, Cuban Miami's nostalgia for the Havana of the past was shakier than it had ever been. The news brought by new arrivals from the island as well as by those who had traveled there on family visits was discouraging in the extreme. Since he had gone to Cuba in 1990 and 1991, Raul Rodriguez, who had traveled there out of love and obsession, found himself the bearer of too much of this bad news. He might spend his days in the high heat of Havana—"The only cool breezes I felt were at Varadero," he once told me ruefully— walking up and down the grand avenues of the bourgeois city taking photos of the houses in which his friends had lived as children, and, when he returned to Miami, he might make copies of these icons of that golden time and, at some considerable expense to himself, deliver as many of these images as there were requests for them. "Ninon," he could be heard to ask on many a quiet weekend morning, "did you give so-and-so her house?"

But though the absence of development in Havana during the

sixties and seventies, the era in which the historic centers of so many Latin American and European cities had been ruined, meant that the facades that Raul photographed so assiduously had been more or less untouched, and, though they uniformly needed a bit of plaster and a coat of paint, it was easy enough to imagine them as they had been in 1959, Raul carried as many disturbing images home with him in his head as he carried heartwarming ones in his camera case. If he could give Sandra Oldham and Tony Quiroga "back" their houses, he was also in a position to tell them just how changed Cuba was. And bricks and mortar were the least of it. The most disturbing news Raul had to impart was that the love for Cuba that stirred so many Miami hearts was not nearly so uniformly shared in Cuba itself.

This, too, made a certain bitter sense. After all, the material difficulties of present-day Cuba, however painful they were to the exiles, only demonstrated the criminality and folly of the Castro regime. In that sense, at least, Cuba's misery was Miami's vindication. Moreover, many in *el exilio* genuinely believed that things would have to get worse before they got better. The vertical position was that the U.S. trade embargo had to be maintained, even though it was clear that to call for this meant that one's own friends and relatives would suffer still further privation. Those who supported this view insisted that were things to improve slightly, as doubtless they would if the American government eased its stance, Castro's grip on power would only be strengthened. They cited the example of the United Nations sanctions against South Africa as a case in which making people's lives worse in the short run had helped bring about change over the longer term. And they were consistent. Congressman Torricelli's legislation, so enthusiastically supported by the Cuban-American National Foundation, called for a ban on all transfers to Cuba with the exception of food, clothing, and medicine. Under these provisions, it would have been illegal for a Cuban-American family in Hialeah or Kendall to even send a toaster or a fan to a relative in East Havana or Santiago de Cuba.

There were, of course, dissenting voices in Cuban Miami. Arturo Vilar was a former newspaperman who now advised businesses about opportunities in various sectors of the Cuban economy. He was in many ways a typical member of the high-bourgeois exile, having lost everything to the revolution. Now, however, his dreams of return, his continuing sense of being a Cuban exile and not either a Cuban-American from Miami or the resident of Madrid that he had been in the sixties, led him not to verticality but to the view that only a reconciliation between the exile and the regime would allow people like himself to return to Havana. In other words, he was for dialogue, and, like Francisco Aruca, whom he knew well, he was much resented for it. People said he was really advising companies on how to do business with the Castro government, a violation of American law. Vilar denied it. But that he was resolutely *dialogero* he did not deny, though, unlike his friend Aruca, he expressed his opinions with sad self-deprecation. When Raul Rodriguez once asked him whether he would go back to Cuba if he could, Vilar smiled sadly. "Oh, yes," he said. "I'd go back. They fucked me over, the revolutionaries. But I'd go back in a minute if I could."

Even Vilar, however, was quick to acknowledge that most people in Cuban Miami were firm supporters of the embargo. "Personally, I don't understand it," he said. "It may be emotional on my part, but when I travel to Cuba, and I run into people who need *everything,* I just can't justify continuing the sanctions, let alone tightening them. I tell myself that I shouldn't be so emotional, but then I think, 'Why not? I'm a human being. And besides, what is this feeling I have for Cuba anyway if it is not something emotional?' It's a painful feeling. These days, knowing how hard things have become in Cuba. I have started to have a rough time enjoying all the things that I have here in Miami. It's not so bad when I'm alone, but when I'm with a group of people, at a dinner, say, with all the food and drink that we Cubans consume on such occasions, I often feel like gagging. I look at the table and I imagine the bare tables of friends in Miramar. We should be sharing our bounty with them, not pressuring the U.S. government to take away what little they have."

But, of course, the people at the Foundation who were pressing for even more restrictions also believed they were acting out of love for Cuba. As Congressman Torricelli put it, the point of a more strictly enforced embargo was to "shorten the suffering of the Cuban people by isolating Castro and forcing him out." Nor was this view restricted to people who had left the island immediately after the revolution. To the contrary, some of the strongest support for the ultravertical position came from those who had come to South Florida since Mariel. A Foundation executive like Rene Jose Silva was being commonsensical when he told an interviewer that he found "a greater affinity for people who have left Cuba recently." In part, of course, his words were one more emblem of the breakup of the exile. People in Miami took Cuban culture for granted, he complained. But Silva was also right to suggest that the intransigent positions of the Foundation coincided with the gloomy sense of so many recent arrivals from the island that force was the only method of unseating Fidel Castro, and that to temporize with the regime in fact guaranteed its survival. As for reconciliation, the very idea was particularly repellent for those whose memories of Cuba were fresh, and as yet untouched by either life in *el exilio* or life in America.

Even Arturo Vilar, though he might yearn for some breakthrough toward understanding between what he often liked to refer to as "the two Cubas," did not really expect his friends and acquaintances in Miami to share his feeling that the disparity between the lives people led in South Florida and the conditions those who had never left the island were now being forced to endure was more troubling even than Fidel Castro's continued rule. In any case, Vilar seemed persuaded that the continuation of the embargo would have the opposite of the desired effect; that anti-Americanism, not antigovernment feeling, would be the inevitable result in Cuba when Congressman Torricelli's Cuban Democracy Act became law. "There needs to be a synthesis between the exile and the island," Vilar told me over a lunch in a Spanish restaurant in Coral Gables called the Cenador de la Villa, where the richness of the food and the lavishness of the presentation would, in fact, have engendered a certain sense of guilt in a person far less committed than Vilar. "But if things continue to deteriorate in Cuba, I just don't see how that meeting can ever occur. The last few times I've been in Havana, I've been overwhelmed by the increasing hostility toward the exiles. People either want to come here or else they dislike us, or, human nature being what it is, feel both things, But when they hear that people in South Florida—Cubans like themselves—want the embargo continued, they can't understand what's going on. The hostility of the U.S. government is one thing. But to know that one's privations are counted as an accomplishment by one's relatives? That's incredibly bitter.''

The problem was that, whatever Vilar might wish, it was also incredibly Cuban. Historically, the notion that one should compromise when fighting for a just cause had, for obvious reasons, had no place in the nineteenth-century wars of independence out of whose experience both Cuba's heroic myths and its political vocabulary had been forged. An episode like the "protest of Baraguá,'' in which Maceo had refused a perfectly reasonable offer of a negotiated surrender to the Spaniards, had been more marking than the actual outcome of the incident, in which Maceo finally gave in and, under safe-conduct, quietly boarded a ship bound for Jamaica and exile. And if the streets of Havana were full of references to this heroic verticality, *el exilio,* too, exemplified a similar spirit. The true Cuban patriot, José Martí had insisted, must be as "prickly as a porcupine, and as upright as a pine tree.'' This was the attitude the eminent exile historian Carlos Ripoll had summed up in a famous essay on the Apostle of Cuban independence that he had entitled "The Noble Intransigence of José Martí.'' That intransigence could be encountered in a Communist slogan like "Socialism or Death''—what, after all, could that possibly mean after the fall of Communism except death, however heroic?—or in the exile insistence that there could be no dialogue, let alone compromise, with the dictator. "We want no compromise,'' Torricelli had insisted in a speech to a cheering Miami crowd, "we want a free Cuba now!''

When liberal Miami Cubans jeered, *"Castro y Mas Canosa, la misma cosa,''* "Castro and Mas Canosa, the same thing,'' they were usually referring to the dictatorial ambitions they discerned in the chairman of the Cuban-American National Foundation.

But whether these similarities were real or not, there was a sense in which all Cuban politicians, whether Communist or capitalist, on the island or in the exile, had been unable to extricate themselves either psychologically or rhetorically from the burden of "noble intransigence." Fidel Castro had bragged that he was going to create the new man. Now, the Cuban economy lay in shambles and the only way out that the Maximum Leader could see was to restore the very tourist sector whose abolition had been one of the revolution's proudest accomplishments. Meanwhile, the exile had dreamed of restoring the Cuba of the past, and in 1992 it was faced with an island that had changed out of all recognition, and a younger generation whose allegiance to the cause could no longer be counted on. When he was growing up, Rene Silva admitted unhappily, too many young Cuban-Americans seemed mainly interested in "making money and having a large car or something."

But even those whose principal ambition was, as Silva had put it, to "get ahead professionally" tended to bridle when their illusions about the island were challenged. They might disagree about the embargo—whatever the Foundation might claim, there was a substantial minority that had qualms about tightening it—and, however quietly, have distanced themselves from the passions of *el tema*. But like American Jews, who were usually far more pious about Israel than Israelis were, Cuban exiles liked to imagine that the patriotism of Cubans on the island was as strong as ever. And it was this illusion that it was Raul Rodriguez's unhappy duty to dispel. For him to bring a woman like Marian Prio Odio, the daughter of Carlos Prío Socarrás, president of Cuba from 1948 to 1952, and the man who would have been the head of the revolutionary junta had the Bay of Pigs invasion succeeded, pictures of intramural Havana was one thing. For Raul to tell her, at a FACE lunch in Coconut Grove, that during his December 1991 trip to Havana he had met two adolescent boys from good families whose first private words to him had been "Cuba is shit" was quite another. It was as if he had kicked her in the solar plexus.

"They meant the regime," she said, as the color returned to

her face. "Raul, you know it's the lives people have been forced to live under Castro that makes them speak in this demented way."

It was a plea as much as it was an assertion. Marian Prio Odio had never been back to Havana. Her husband, Cesar, was now the City of Miami manager, effectively the second most important elected official in Greater Miami. She lived a Cuban-American life, a successful and public-spirited one, but like Raul, she still grieved. Clearly, the last thing she wanted to hear was that the object of her longing did not inspire the same devotion—indeed, that it inspired loathing—in many of those who had remained behind. If Cubans no longer loved Cuba, then what kind of solidarity could there be between the island and the diaspora? And if no such complicity, if only on the level of feeling, existed, then what did it really mean to be Cuban in Miami, or to cherish the hope that one day a divided people could join together again? The prospect was too awful to contemplate, and Marian was not alone, in Cuban Miami as a community or at that FACE luncheon table in particular, in rebelling at the thought.

But Raul only shook his head. When he had first gone to Cuba, he too would have been as shocked as his colleagues on the FACE board to hear Cubans speak with disdain of Cuba. Like them, however deep his loyalty and respect for the United States, he would never love a country as well as he had loved Cuba as both a child in Miramar and an exile in Miami. Before he had returned to Havana, he would have probably shared the consoling assumption that for someone on the island to say he or she hated Cuba was really a disguised way of voicing loathing for what Fidel Castro had done to Cuba. But after four visits over nineteen months, Raul had been disabused of any such notion. By his own admission, he had resisted the bad news at first, but now that he had accepted it, there was no backing away. "No, it was more than that," he replied, at last. "So many young people want nothing to do with Cuba or with being Cuban anymore. That's all over for them now.

"Do you know what the saying is in Havana?" he continued, the misery in his voice as complete as the unhappiness of

Marian's face as she waited for the unwelcome punch line. "In Havana, when you ask a kid, 'What do you want to be when you grow up?,' that kid is likely to answer, 'I want to be either a tourist or a foreigner.' "

"Oh, no Raul," Marian Prio Odio said.

But he was not done. "There are people in Havana," he said, "you can meet them in Miami easily enough, many came at the time of Mariel, who volunteered, *volunteered,* to fight in Angola, not because they were Communists, or because they were forced to go, but because they were literally willing to do anything to leave Cuba, even risk killing or being killed. Imagine, they thought it might be better to take the chance of dying in some godforsaken bit of Africa just for the opportunity to see some other part of the world than their own country."

And, along with her friends, Marian Prio Odio stood there rapt, hearing every word that Raul Rodriguez, usually so conciliatory and, always, such a lover of Cuba, had tossed at her, tossed like a live grenade at her. "I never believed such a thing was possible," she sighed. She was not alone. In Miami, in 1992, no unconditional lover of Cuba was yet alone. And yet Miami could not afford to imagine such things. As Zionists had, to their cost, imagined a Palestine without Arabs, so *el exilio* had concocted a Cuba in which there was tyranny, but where, once Castro had been removed, nothing would separate Cubans from one another again. To have to fight Americans for the right to love Cuba, or to feel Cuban, whatever passport one carried, was one thing. But to discover that the Cuba one loved was full of Cubans who might not share this passion, that was unendurable. And yet with every word issuing from Raul's mouth, the carefully constructed, lovingly maintained image of unity and concord began to fall apart. In its place, rootlessness loomed, and, even more than rootlessness, marginality. For without Cuba, Cuban-Americans would simply be an interesting and influential American ethnic group, their dreams and obsessions only some of the many dreams, many obsessions that would vie for a hearing in polyglot, multicultural America. As much as anything, the fear of assimilating was, quite literally, a fear of getting lost, of seeing oneself not as one wanted to be seen but as others actually saw one.

For all the materialistic impulses for which they were so frequently taxed, Cuban Miamians of Raul and Marian's generation wanted far more than comfort. Above all, they wanted to regain that sense of belonging that they had enjoyed as children in Havana, and, despite the degree to which, though it was not really an enclave, it was possible to live in Miami as if it were an enclave, they had never regained since. If they could not make their dreams come true, at least they did not want to see them proven false. They were so bedazzling, those dreams. At a conference on business opportunities in post-Castro Cuba, I met an architect named Jose Castro, a friend of Raul and Ninon's, who described his version of that ubiquitous Miami Cuban dream. "I found myself entering the river of Matanzas," he recounted, "in some kind of glass-bottom boat. It was magical. My childhood, oh, my happy childhood, came flooding back to me. It was marvelous. I realized that I knew perfectly how to navigate around the town, and I arrived, without any strain, at my uncle's house. I went up to the door, opened it, and went in. I was at home. Then I woke up, and for a long time I was still possessed by those wonderful feelings, by the sense of belonging, of fitting in at last. I think you would say that I've done well here, but never in America—and I have an American lover, you know— have I felt that sense I had in that dream."

What Jose Castro could only find in his dreams—he had not traveled back to Cuba, nor did he think that were Castro to fall he was likely to return to the island to live—Raul had at times been able to find during his brief sojourns in Havana. It galled him, he said, that he had to apply for a visa to visit "my own country," and although this was partly due to his anger over the Cuban government's inconsistency toward the exiles (since, although Raul had to apply for a visa, he was forbidden to travel on his American passport), what he objected to mainly was the idea that he could ever, no matter how long he lived in Miami, be a foreigner in Cuba. "I'm frightened, of course," he admitted, "but never for a moment do I have the sense of being a stranger.

The names make sense; the place makes sense in ways that, at least for me, Miami never will. Even today, when I go to a rich person's house, on some street like North Bay Road in Miami Beach, even if I greatly admire the architecture, I'll find myself thinking, 'It's wonderful, but it's not my idea of a house.' Whereas in Cuba, even when the paint is peeling off the walls, as it usually is, and the runners are chipped, I have just as unforced a sense of being at ease. It's not that I want to feel this way. It's almost instinctive.''

Raul Rodriguez had known he wanted to be an architect since he was seven years old and one of his uncles commissioned a small, modernist apartment complex in Miramar. The young Raul—he too was called Ruly then—had hung around during the construction, entranced by everything about the process. To some extent, his memories of childhood were as centered around buildings as most people's were centered around food. But as the memories of Havana buildings, and his effort, during his trips to the island, to take photos of as many of them as possible, had formed, apart from the chance to see the few family members who remained, the affective core of his pilgrimages to Havana, so an architectural debate in Miami, as much as if not more than what he had seen on the island, had confirmed his increasingly grim sense of what conflicts lay in store between the exiles who might choose to return and those Cubans who had remained. It was a parochial Miami story, and yet its effect on Raul had been profound.

One afternoon, Raul and Tony Quiroga had gone to a community board meeting in a neighborhood that had once been white and was now almost entirely composed of American blacks and Haitian immigrants. The school board of Miami planned to build a new school building, and Rodriguez and Quiroga were among the firms bidding for the contract. Such meetings in Miami, more often than not, are *pro forma* affairs in which the local community board more or less automatically ratifies the decision of the city commission and the board of education. But this time, Raul and Tony walked into the bitterest of confrontations. On one side of the auditorium were scores of middle-aged white alumni dressed in red school jackets. They were there to demand that the old school building, the one they had attended, sometimes as long as thirty years before and in no case more recently than a decade previously, be preserved. On the other side of the room were row after row of black and Haitian parents, the people whose children now attended the school, who were equally determined that an entirely new facility be built.

"You can have no idea how awful it was," Raul told me later that day. "The whites were there talking about how it was important that Miami preserve its past, that too much had been destroyed already in the city and that it was time to start keeping memories alive rather than paving them over, and that it was a fine building that could easily be restored, a point of view that, from a purely professional, architectural standpoint, I knew that they were right to take. But the black parents took exactly the opposite view. The main thing for them was that a new building would have no associations with the past. 'Those good old days were segregated old days,' one man shouted to cheers and applause. 'and I don't want my kids having any part of it. I want that old building knocked down, because I hate seeing it. Every time I drive by that old school it makes me angry. We weren't allowed in. We had to go somewhere else.' "

By the time Raul and Tony had left the meeting, it had degenerated into name-calling and tears. To an outsider, it had appeared not so much like a conflict between right and wrong as a tragedy in the old-fashioned sense of both sides being right. In any case, in a Miami where budget constraints probably meant that no decision would be taken for some time, neither side had carried the day. And Raul, who was both dedicated to historic preservation and at the same time very much alive to the mistreatment so many blacks still received in Miami, remained unsure which position was preferable. But as he drove home, what obsessed him was not so much what he had witnessed, and what the dispute symbolized about the state of race relations in Miami, so much as the fact that similar conflicts were likely, even if Castro fell without bloodshed and the Cuban economy made the most miraculous of recoveries, to bedevil the island in the post-Communist period. "That scene," he said, "reminded me of how our Miami Cuban good memories of the buildings of Havana and the life that we led in them are bound to come into conflict with the bad memories and bad feelings of those who stuck it out. I kept running the tape of some future meeting of preservationists going on and on, as I do so much, about the beauty of the architecture and the possibility of keeping things more or less intact, while a Havana audience hoots and jeers, and tells us, 'What we want is air-conditioning. That's what we've been missing all these years, while you been pining away for the sea breezes from off the Malecón!''

Oddly enough, though, while Raul, who had been back to Cuba, was full of foreboding, it was on the level of being able to fulfill the material dreams of a people deprived of nearly every creature comfort from automobiles to air conditioners for so long that many Miami Cubans remained as confident as ever. The collapse of Communism as a world economic system had reinforced their faith in the virtues of the market economy, and the contrast between their own prosperity and the inability of the Castro government even to keep the electricity running in Havana twenty-four hours a day (in 1992, selective blackouts had begun to be imposed on a regular basis) made them confident that Cubans on the island would quickly come around to the exile's way of doing things. That was what Felix Rodriguez had meant when he insisted that it wasn't hard to trade in a bad life for a good one. In the end, it seemed, Cuban Miami's strongest hope lay not in its nostalgia, however profound, for the Havana of yesterday, but in its mercantile expectations of restoring the Cuba of tomorrow. To be sure, the love of Cuba came before everything else, and that love was based on memory. But those memories had fused, over the decades, with Cuban Miami's other love, which was business. It was as if the exiles were saying, 'Let us return, and we will restore Cuba to the prosperous image we have conserved of her.' Viewed from this perspective, not only was there nothing wrong, as liberal Cubans tended to allege, in conflating *el tema* and *el negocio,* but, rather, the building materials and investment credits that would be Cuba's salvation in a post-Castro era would come from those who, as Cristina Garcia had put it, had been "dreaming in Cuban" for so long.

Certainly, the language of dreaming and the language of national reconstruction were often hard to distinguish in Cuban Miami in the early nineties. People oscillated from reminiscence to business plan, from a narrative of loss to the prospect of psychic closure. Sandra Gonzalez-Levy, the vice-president of the Greater Miami Chamber of Commerce, whom I had met through Raul and who was one of the most eloquent proselytizers for the view that the exile would make the crucial difference in a capitalist Cuba, exemplified this attitude. "A future Cuban government," she told me, "is going to have to look for both investors and resources. I think Cuba will eventually be a very interesting investment opportunity for any business interest, whatever its nationality. But in the short run, they're going to have to deal with the exile. We're the ones who already have an emotional investment in Cuba."

If Gonzalez-Levy spoke of reconstructing the island's economy, she was, by her own ready admission, also speaking of bringing her own life back into balance. "I left something behind when my father brought us into exile. There's a part of me I haven't been able to discover. I need to find out about it, whether it's good or bad." And from longing she moved to faith. "We're going to be able to reconstruct some of our memories," she told me firmly. "I was only a little girl when we left, but I think we exiles will be able to go back, see Havana, and be proud of it. There must be people there who still have memories of what it was like before. Anyhow, I know we can remake Old Havana. We'll restore the city to its heyday, bring it back as we remember it."

By then, Gonzalez-Levy's enthusiasm was running away with her and she knew it. With a laugh, she said, "Well, maybe just the opportunity to go back will make us whole. There has to be a happy medium. We are hungry for the Cuban past, and they're eager for America. We'll blend well together, we'll compromise." I must have raised an eyebrow. "Yes," said Sandra Gonzalez-Levy, "I know. We Cubans don't compromise. But I tell you, we won't be divided again, whatever happens."

She had been joking when she said Cubans didn't compromise,

but, in fact, the assumption that Cubans had a choice between a Cubanity based on Communism and a Cubanity based on commerce was no joke. That a close association between business and politics should have existed was predictable enough. Not only was success in commerce accorded pride of place in a mercantile culture like that of Cuban Miami, but the idea of capitalist success, far from being only implicitly related to politics, as it was in most developed countries, had stood for Cuban exiles in South Florida as part and parcel of their struggle against Fidel Castro. Even to make money was to be able to rebuild some simulacrum of what the more prosperous exiles had possessed in Miramar or El Vedado. And to make money was to demonstrate that exile had had its triumphs as well as its defeats. It was this success in business, a success attained against all odds, that had played such a central role in the exile's ability to keep its hopes alive. For a Sandra Gonzalez-Levy to accept that the reality of Cuba might not match up to her expectations would be to repudiate her memories. By the same token, to really accept that the Cuban future might not be promising entailed the still more radical demand that the exiles repudiate the meaning they had assigned to their own success in the United States. For it was an article of faith in Cuban Miami that the community's economic prosperity was overwhelmingly the result of its will, drive, and character. Having been history's victims once, after 1959 the Cuban diaspora had fashioned its own destiny.

Hadn't the Cubans come to Miami with nothing but their wounds and their business acumen and, within a generation, built a thriving community within a booming city? Conditions in a post-Castro Cuba could not be bleaker than they had been for the first refugees to reach Dade County in the early sixties. Men who had been bank presidents in Havana had eked out livings as bookkeepers then, and talented doctors and lawyers—the cream of the University of Havana—had swept up in fast-food restaurants, grateful to get the work while they struggled to learn English and to requalify in their specialties. For Cuban-Americans over forty in Miami, whatever their political views, even the signs of the city's prosperity could call forth memories of that shabby, deflated time. Having lived in Havana, in the words of a

Cuban government tourist brochure of the late thirties, "like plutocrats on the salaries of bureaucrats," the exiles had fallen through layer after class layer as they tried to remake lives in America. That they had subsequently recouped this status, and, for that matter, often improved upon it, only drew off part of the sting. One never knew when the residue would make itself felt. One evening in Miami in the summer of 1986, during the first prolonged period I spent in the city, I went to a dinner party at a Miami Beach hotel given by a friend named Danilo Bardisa, the man who had first introduced me to South Florida. At a certain point, the wine having caught up with me, I got up to go to the lavatory, and asked Danny where it was. He pointed toward an interior stair and, before dropping his arm, grabbed my wrist. "Take a good look while you're in there," he said. "My father was the attendant there in '60 and '61."

Bardisa senior had moved on, of course, as had most people in Cuban Miami. But it was by no means as easy to jettison one's memories as it was to exchange a mop and a pail for a dentist's white smock or an Armani suit. If Cuban Miami's lingering bitterness toward the non-Cuban city derived, in part at least, from this collective memory of having sweated for it as a servant class, however brief such service had been, and if this resentment was compounded by the suspicion that native-born Americans actually didn't like Cubans very much—even Felix Rodriguez, career CIA official though he was, admitted offhandedly that one of the reasons that made him eager to return to Cuba was that "no one can look down on you in your own country"—the exile's triumphalist expectations about what it could hope to accomplish on the island after Castro fell derived from its memories of having succeeded so completely. It was all very well for outsiders to point out that the business skills the Cuban middle class had possessed far outweighed their lack of capital, or to note that the new arrivals had been perfectly positioned to capitalize on the economic boom that, in the seventies, had lifted not only Miami, but cities all over the American Sunbelt from Orlando to Phoenix. The fact remained that most observers at the time would have bet on Cuban failure, not Cuban success. Indeed, in the early sixties, the U.S. government had been so worried about a

dependent population of Cubans that it had put tremendous pressure on families to leave South Florida.

But they had returned, and they had prospered. This they took
to be proof that it was the exile that represented the deepest, most
authentic Cubanness. When Rene Silva asserted in an interview
that there seemed to "be something in the Cuban nature that
creates entrepreneurs," and went on to say that "the dream of
every Cuban [is] to have a business; have his own business and
his own destiny in his hands," he was in effect saying that Fidel
Castro had perverted the Cuban essence when he had imposed
socialism on the island. By the same token, if the exile were to
aid in restoring capitalism, they were not simply, whether out of
love or self-interest, helping to set up a better economic structure,
but were also helping their fellow Cubans rediscover their own
natures. How could it fail? Cubans on the island were simply
being asked to live more comfortable lives in a situation in which
they could be truer to themselves. For its part, the exile, by being
able to return to the island, if probably not to live then at least,
to use the intentionally vague formulation current in Miami in the
early nineties, to "help," could finally hope to see its wounds
heal, its devotion to the idea of Cuba rewarded.

This was not to say that people in Miami had not, beginning in
1989, also genuinely expected to make money out of the economic transformation of Cuba. The number of seminars and position papers concerning the switch to capitalism, not to mention
the competition, the existence of which was officially denied by
all concerned, for franchises in everything from consumer elec-
tronics to McDonald's outlets, testified to that. There was a ru-
mor in Miami in 1992 that Felix Rodriguez was trying to get a
Holiday Inn franchise in Havana—both the corporation and the
shadow warrior himself denied it. "I get letters every day from
Cubans in the U.S. who want to go back to Cuba eventually,"
said Barry Kisch, international licensing manager for McDonald's, but, he added gnomically, "they know that nothing will
happen until it's ready to happen."

The truth was that many Miami Cubans did think the time was
almost ripe. In November 1991, the Florida Bar sent out a mail-

ing that stated this expectation in no uncertain terms. "Anticipating the post-Castro era," the notice began, "the Bar's International Law Section has established a Cuban Affairs Committee. [It] is organizing a symposium on Post-Castro Cuba, Dealing with the Transition (Legal, Commercial, and Economic Issues), scheduled for May 7 and 8, 1992, at the Inter-Continental Hotel, Miami, Florida." These were hardly the only contingency plans. From zoning lawyers to steamship companies, and from the Latin Builders' Association to *The Miami Herald,* which in 1992 set up a special unit prepared to cover every aspect of Fidel Castro's fall and its aftermath, Miamians, non-Cubans as well as Cubans, were waiting for the post-Communist era to begin. The economic rationale was almost as self-evident as the sentimental one. Miami itself, particularly after the devastation caused by Hurricane Andrew, would be an economic basket case for the foreseeable future. The real possibilities for the kind of untrammeled growth that had fueled the South Florida boom of the seventies and early eighties would, in the nineties, be found south of the Strait if they existed at all. "Think of it," a prominent Miami lawyer remarked to me during the morning coffee break after the opening session of the "Dealing with the Transition" conference. "There's a whole country down there just waiting to be brought up to code."

For the most part, the importance of Cuba as a market was taken for granted, as was the assumption that it would be Floridians, particularly Miami Cubans, who would be best able to take advantage of the island's potential. As George Harper, the Cuban-born American lawyer who had organized the conference at the Inter-Continental, put it, Cuba offered businessmen "eleven million consumers who for thirty years have had little in the way of new or modernized housing, appliances, consumer goods, or automobiles; [the island had] beautiful beaches and mountains, located close to the U.S.A.; the world's largest reserves of nickel and other minerals, with an estimated value of two hundred billion dollars; fertile topsoil and a favorable climate for coffee, citrus, and other agricultural products; [and] investors and workers with the means, talent, and desire to export or invest in Cuba;

some on a large scale, some on a small scale." Most important of all, Harper emphasized, was the fact that so many of these prospective investors "have the same cultural background, ethnicity, language, and history as those now living in Cuba."

That, at least, was the hope. And few disagreed. Even Raul Rodriguez, though he had come to doubt the commonality of worldview between the Cubans on the island and the Cubans of the exile, and, having observed people in Havana keeping American cars from the early fifties going on little more than ingenuity, did not believe that people who had learned to wheel and deal on the black market in order to survive necessarily needed lessons in entrepreneurship from people who, except during the power outage that had followed Hurricane Andrew and had only lasted a few weeks in middle-class areas of Miami, never spent more than a day or two without air-conditioning, tended to believe that many in the exile stood to make a great deal of money. One person who disagreed, though, was Raul's friend Michael Lewis, an American married to a Cuban woman who ran an energetic South Florida business weekly, *Miami Today*. "There will be people who get rich in a post-Castro island," he told me over lunch, "but I would guess that most of them will not be local people. I can easily imagine a Coca-Cola, or an AT&T, making money, and, of course, I'm sure the great business dynasties of prerevolutionary Cuba, families like the Bacardis and the Gomez Menas, will at least want to get their property back. But for the small-time investor, despite all the knocks we've taken, I still think Miami will be a safer bet for the near term."

He continued, "Of course, everything depends on what time frame you're considering. In the real long term, anything is possible, but right now I just can't see that the prospects on the island are particularly bright. The things that Cuba produced before the revolution are not nearly such valuable commodities as they were back in the fifties. Tobacco won't be what it was before. What restaurant will let you smoke a cigar nowadays? And surely sugar won't be what it was before. These are products that a lot of middle-class people are trying to give up. Even in Miami, among the Cuban population, the amount of sugar younger people consume is a fraction of what their parents take in."

I asked Lewis about the prospects for tourism, that lodestar which, when all was said and done, was the sector that most people in Miami (and, of course, nowadays, in Havana as well) tended to single out as the major source of capital for Cuba's future economic development. But Lewis only shook his head.

"I don't mean to be a contrarian," he said, "but I don't believe in that solution either. There are other resort islands now, thanks to Fidel Castro. You could almost say that they developed because of him, couldn't you? In the fifties, all those resorts in Puerto Rico, the Dominican Republic, along the Atlantic coast of Mexico, and in the rest of the Caribbean barely existed. Now, the money is pouring in, far more money than is going to come to Cuba. The people who own these places are not just going to roll over and play dead after Castro falls. And while I'm sure that at first there will be a lot of visitors going to Havana from Miami— the Cuban-Americans, I mean—the real question is how often they will return and how much money they will spend on each trip."

For Lewis, there was a real confusion between the projections being made concerning Cuban-American investment and Cuban-American tourism on the one hand, and what he called "real" or competitive tourism on the other. After Cuban-Americans had made a trip back, and had distributed gifts to their relatives, he reasoned, the traffic would slacken. "Even leaving out the question of whether even the ten or fifteen percent of the exiles who say they'll return to live will actually go, will the visitors be able to go back and forth every week? Every month? How can they possibly afford to? We have a recession here in Miami."

In any event, tourism was, in Lewis's view, a poor way to fuel any growing economy. "Let's say there are half a million people in Miami who identify deeply with Cuba," he said. "And let's say that a hundred thousand of them—that's a lot, incidentally; one in five—go back regularly. That means that you are expecting the expenditures of a hundred thousand people to underwrite the living expenses of more than ten million people. How can that work? When I was a young man, I used to work on Mackinac Island, the resort near Detroit. It got six hundred thousand tourists every summer, and their revenues only had to support nine hundred full-time residents and the couple of thousand people who worked there during the season. The numbers just don't add up for Cuba. Besides, will people really want to go? I'm not Cuban, but I'm married to a Cuban and it's a country I care about. But what I've seen of the place in Raul and Ninon's slides doesn't make me want to go there. When you take a holiday, you want it to be a holiday. You don't want to see dilapidated buildings and suffering people, even if you are related to them." He paused. "Maybe particularly if you're related to them.

"It's not that I question Raul or Ninon's commitment," he went on, "or their view of Cuba, any more than I question my own sense of Miami. But I do know that they have their memories to fall back on and that those memories are positive ones. Havana is bound to look different to someone who was poor there—and remember, for starters, everyone who stayed is poor by U.S. standards except a few officials—just as Miami looks far different to someone who grew up in Liberty City than it does to me. And while I'm an optimist about Miami's future, I don't think our economy is going to get so strong that all the Cuban-American professionals I know are going to have so much extra cash that they will be able to work on the island on what will basically be a *pro bono* basis. Just spending the money to buy the things their relatives will need—and a lot of those relatives are going to be coming to Miami, by the way—is going to drain off their bank accounts. As for the small investor, where are the equity guarantees going to come from? And on the island, who is going to have the money to buy all those dishwashers and burgers? A McDonald's hamburger costs a day's pay in Moscow.

"Everyone here, from the Foundation to the university think tanks, talks about the East German model. We now know that East Germany's a disaster, that trying to pay for unification has almost ruined the Common Market. And at least East Germany had West Germany. Cuba doesn't have the United States; it has the Cuban-American community; it has Miami. Can Miami pay for the environmental cleanup that will have to take place? What about the basic infrastructure? You can't support a nation on your childhood memories."

But, of course, that was exactly what so many Cuban Miamians thought. They had jumbled so many things together. Childhood memories were being conflated with present-day realities; questions of family reunification were being confused with those of the island's merits as a tourist destination; and the money that might be made in Cuba was rarely differentiated from the monies that Cuba could be expected to hold on to. "Remember," Michael Lewis had said before we parted, "Central America supports a lot of banana companies and that certainly has not meant anything very positive for the people who live in the region." What Lewis was saying was that the fine Cuba of the exile's memories was gone for good, and that even a change of regime would not restore it. In sentimental terms, many Cubans might feel as close to Havana as ever, but practically, despite the fusion of a psychological and material cargo cult that was contained within the fantasy of return, practical questions were pulling them in a very different direction. And while they might have wished it otherwise, the end of socialism in Cuba, when and if it came, did not mean the end of the exile. For by 1992, that condition had itself become a dream—a very particular, haunting Miami dream.

But most people in Miami had grown so accustomed to their fantasy that they had come to believe in it as passionately when they were awake, and, ostensibly, thinking in the most hardheaded, practical terms, as they would have had they been asleep. Only the young quarreled with the basic premises of return in any unremitting way, the young and a man I shall call Juan Carlos. He was the only person in Cuban Miami who spoke to me on the condition that he not be identified. And when he had finished I understood why, for his view would have made so much of his family and social life impossible. Why, feeling the way he did, he continued to live in Miami, I never found out. He was rich, and could have gone anywhere. All he would say was "I want to see the end of this story. I want to be here when the wake-up call comes."

But about the illusions of his fellow Cubans, he was scathing. "All these people with their fantasies of return," he said, "all the Mas Canosas, the Maria Cristina Herreras, the Left and the Right, the top and the bottom—it's an illusion. They're Americans, or they've become Americans anyway. And these are American fantasies; it's so American to think that you can be whatever you want to be, that there isn't the slightest bit of difference between dreams and realities, between what you want and what you are given. People here say, 'Hey, we didn't deserve our fate; it's so unfair that we were forced to leave Cuba.' Can you imagine? They're right, of course. It was unfair, like nature. But they want to say that what happened is *un*natural"—he stressed the first syllable—"just as modern people really believe that mortality is unnatural, and that somehow what happened can be undone. It's so American. 'I'll wake up, and instead of being a middle-aged Miami Cuban, I'll be a child on Varadero beach, walking with my nanny along the shoreline.' "

He smiled. "I used to live at Varadero, you know," Then he caught himself. "You see," he said, "I'm not immune to these tribal myths either. None of us are. And maybe we shouldn't be. Today, the United States is not a country, it's a world. Within it, each tribe needs its dreams and its dogmas, however farfetched. By that standard, we Cubans are realists. None of us are going back, you'll see, no one but a magnate here and retiree there will go back. But our dream gave us strength when we needed it, and if we can't quite let go, is that really so terrible? Actually, what I really fear is what will happen when people can go back. The psychiatrists will make a killing when people learn that the island is closer in atmosphere to Haiti than to Coral Gables. That's when the trouble will begin, after Castro falls, I mean, and the exile's bill starts falling due."

He laughed again, mirthlessly. "The lucky ones," he told me, "are the ones who have paid in advance."

10

By 1992, Raul Rodriguez had been paying in advance for more than twelve years. In 1980, he and Ninon had been in the first wave of the first Cuban Miamians to take advantage of the renewed possibility of visiting Havana that had been the most promising side effect of the brief period of "dialogue" between the U.S. and Cuba. They were both thirty-two years old then, and only at the beginning of their careers. Raul was a junior member of a large architectural firm; Ninon had started teaching at Miami-Dade Community College two years before. For them to have made the trip at all—they were, after all, not political people in any real sense, nor were they involved in some professional or academic study of the island that might have given their trip some tenuous legitimacy in the minds of their friends and family in Miami—was an almost foolhardy thing to do at the time. Raul's mother wept. The couple's friends gossiped behind their backs, and, when they returned, eyed them suspiciously for a time. Even much later, after many thousands of Cuban Miamians had taken the same journey, Raul knew that at any social gathering or professional meeting he attended, there was a fair chance that someone would reproach him for his repeated journeys to the island. "I'm not too crazy about people going down there," a lawyer named Ernesto de la Fe declared edgily after Raul had given a speech on historic preservation in Havana at the Post-Castro Cuba conference. And Raul only nodded politely. He had heard such remarks too often in the past to be disturbed by them still.

Raul also knew that while many people in Cuban Miami objected to his having gone to Cuba, those same people rarely turned down an invitation to spend an evening at his house looking at the slides he had taken of the city during his stays there. The same Ernesto de la Fe who had reproached him for going had reminisced only a few moments before about a house in Havana that his uncle had owned, and had even asked Raul whether he had an image of it in his collection. Raul had replied that he did, and that anytime de la Fe wanted he could have a copy of the slide. "I probably have a lot of pictures of houses your relatives lived in," Raul had said gently. "Come over some evening. I'd be glad to show them to you."

Of course, in offering to show the photographs of Havana that he had amassed during his visits there to Ernesto de la Fe, or for that matter, to even less sympathetic interlocutors, Raul was doing much more than either attempting to defuse the inevitable criticisms of his trips or providing his fellow Cuban Miamians with actual views of what their hazily remembered family homes and old neighborhoods now looked like. Doubtless that was part of the story. For Raul, with his Catholic schoolboy's tropism toward public service—from the Metro-Dade Art in Public Places Trust, to FACE, to the South Florida Historical Association, there were few nonprofit groups in Dade County that Raul had refused to serve on when approached, however little he could afford the time—took it as a matter of obligation that when he visited Havana he owed it to his neighbors in Miami to visit their family houses and even seek out their family crypts in the vast, beautiful central cemetery of Havana, the Cementerio de Colón, which, along with La Recoleta in Buenos Aires, was the finest example of southern European funerary architecture in the Americas. He also reveled in the beauty of Havana—"It's a library of architecture," he liked to say—and often contrasted its distinguished buildings, both from the period of the Spanish viceroyalty and from the Le Corbusier–inflected nineteen-fifties, with the conformity and ugliness of Collins Avenue in Miami Beach or the new developments in Coconut Grove or Kendall. But however much Raul might admire the way Havana looked, the pictures he took were more than just a method of appreciating or documenting that beauty. More than anything else, they represented both the idea and the emotion of return.

There is a Virgilio Piñera story, written in the nineteen-forties, about a Cuban farmer who decides that he will consume the mountain standing across the valley from his ranch. This he means literally. So every morning he sets out and, arriving at the mountain's base, falls to his knees and begins to swallow everything—dirt, roots, grass, pebbles—that he can stuff into his mouth. At the end of each day, exhausted, the farmer returns home. And Piñera ends his tale by portraying the farmer seated on his porch, staring out at the mountain and thinking with satisfaction that, although none of his neighbors seemed aware yet of what was taking place, and, to the casual observer, the mountain looked the same, he could see the progress he was making and knew for certain that the mountain was getting smaller.

The story is an allegory. The farmer is the *guajiro,* the archetypal Cuban of folklore. And the mountain, of course, is Cuba itself. Piñera's own ambivalence about his country is evident. The farmer wants to destroy the mountain, or at least hopes that by shrinking it he will be able to remove its oppressive presence from overshadowing everything else in his field of view. But he also wants to become the mountain. In Piñera's time, the age before political correctness, it was a commonplace that the Ciboney Indians, the original inhabitants of the island, had been cannibals. And Piñera, who would have known this story and reveled in it, makes his farmer, his Ur-Cuban, a cannibal, and his assault on the mountain also an attempt to assimilate its qualities in the way that cannibals were said to eat their opponents' flesh in hope of acquiring their qualities. That either version of the enterprise is hopeless, that, in a sense, there is no coming to terms with Cuba, is a given of the story. Piñera was always a pessimist. But, at the same time, his farmer is the Quixotic Cuban everyman, as nobly intransigent in pursuing his hopeless task as José Martí could have wished.

Because he understood the Cuban character so well, Piñera, had he lived instead of being driven to an early grave by the revolution's cultural bureaucrats, who were unable to stomach the great writer's homosexuality or his aesthete's pessimism, doubtless would have resonated to Raul's picture-taking. For just as the farmer was trying to cram the mountain into his mouth, so, during his stays in Havana, was Raul trying to consume the whole city with his camera. As he drove around in the white Nissan rented from a government tourist agency called Havanautos, Raul carried two cameras—a fine thirty-five-millimeter that he saved for shots he had time to set up and frame properly, and a small, self-focusing Minolta that he could simply point and click. The thirty-five he kept in a case just in back of the gearshift; the little Minolta usually rested on his lap when it wasn't in his hands. Even as one trip succeeded the other, and as Raul grew more and more familiar with the streets of his boyhood—with Paseo, Fifth Avenue, the Malecón, and Avenido de los Presidentes—his desire to accumulate more and more of these plangent souvenirs only seemed to grow stronger. By the fourth trip, he was taking new shots of facades he had already photographed, not because he had forgotten his earlier efforts and was duplicating them inadvertently, but because the act of taking these pictures had never been principally motivated by the desire to compile a record of the city.

Havana's dilapidation may have strengthened his resolve—so many buildings in the old city were, by 1992, being propped up with poles and siding, like ancient trees in a Japanese garden—but the fear that many buildings would not survive much longer was both immeasurably painful to Raul and incidental to his enterprise. Before he left Miami, he would agonize over whether he had brought enough film, and, after he had returned, he would fret until the rolls had been developed and he had ordered them in carousels. Interestingly, I rarely saw Raul focus his camera on a person. The citizens of Havana might appear in the background, and at the beginning and the end of each trip Raul would take a roll of shots of his wife and son posed in front of some Havana monument or in a group shot with relatives who still lived in the city, but it was the architecture that was central. Walking down Paseo, Raul would pause again and again and tell the rest of us in excited tones who had lived in this or that great mansion, when this apartment block had been erected, or who the architect had been. Sometimes he was bitter at what had happened to the buildings of Havana, particularly when the change had taken place after he and Ninon and Ruly had begun making trips to the island. "Shit," he said, with rare bitterness, as he took me to see the old house in Miramar in which he spent his ninth and tenth years, "the palm tree died. It was there when we were here in 1980, the last thing that was left of the old place that really looked the way it did back then." He paused, mastering his emotions. "That makes one more thing the Cuban government owes me," he said with a smile, "a palm tree . . . and ten million pesos."

He pulled up to the curb, behind a green 1955 Chevy with its left front door missing that was up on blocks. The front garden was a riot. He walked in. Raul's old house, it turned out, had been turned into a center where botany was taught to elementary school students. Where Raul remembered a dining room, there were stools and tiny desks, and a blackboard with beautiful images of ferns drawn in colored chalk. Behind the house, the structure of a pool still stood, although it was empty, and almost up to its edge there were row after row of hydroponic planters. "One time, my brother Frankie fell into that pool and almost drowned," Raul said, drinking in the view. "My school was just across the street, La Salle de Miramar. But I couldn't wait to get home, to this backyard and this house."

"Comrades?"

Standing framed in the rear door was a very slim old man in a peasant smock. He held a trowel in his hand and was eyeing us with caution.

"I knocked," Raul said. "There was no answer and so we came in. I used to live in this house long ago, before the revolution."

The old man relaxed, and, his gait surprisingly firm, strode across the yard toward us. "I'm Guillermo Coto," he said, shaking Raul's hand. "I run this school. It's used to teach children about the flora of Cuba." We began to walk amid the planters. "Take a look, *compañera*," he said to Ninon, "look at everything if you like. I hope you don't mind that I call you comrade. We say comrade proudly here in Cuba now, because we know we are creating a just society." Ninon flinched. "Well," the old man said, having caught her look, "if we are wrong time will surely let us know. But for now, in the few years that are left to me I am trying to teach botany in Marxist-Leninist terms. For me, it's a wonderful way to finish out my life. I'm a Costa Rican, you know, but I always sympathized with Cuba. Even when I had more hope for my own country, I dreamed of coming here, of living in Havana."

"I can well understand that," Raul said.

Coto peered at him. Raul shifted his feet nervously, then stiffened and stared back. "We had heard a member of the Partagas family had lived in this house, but we weren't sure," the old man said. "But you had gone a long time before we took over this place as a space for our pedagogic botanical garden. It was a carpentry shop before that, you know. But then we acquired it, without violence to anyone, I might add, and have since tried to give this house a destiny that we thought would be appropriate and not dishonorable for it."

"I'm glad if it's of use," Raul said gravely, and we took our leave.

At Fifth Avenue, as we drove back toward the hotel, we passed the stark, Mussoliniesque 1930s church where Raul's parents had worshiped and in which both he and his two brothers had been baptized. "They were a little perfunctory about religion," he admitted as we drove by. "I guess I'm the same way." And during the rest of that afternoon, at any rate, Raul's religion was Havana itself. After a quick lunch at the hotel, he announced suddenly that he wanted to go to the Old City again. "Oh, no," Ruly said, "I hate that," but his father was already out of the hotel dining room and into the lobby, pulling out his car keys as he went. We drove down to the Plaza de Armas, and walked first to the Palace of the Captains General, the Cuban seat of government during colonial times. Inside, in an upstairs room that, unlike every other museum space in the city, was luxuriously air-conditioned, we walked in silence past the frayed battle standards of Cuba's wars of independence. Leaving the building, we walked down to El Templete, the early-nineteenth-century neoclassical monument commemorating Havana's founding. Raul stared at its facade for a long moment and then said, under his breath, "I would have loved this life if I'd been given the chance."

From the Plaza de Armas, Raul led us south onto Obispo Street, in pre-Castro days the Wall Street of Cuba. We passed the old Royal Bank of Canada and Trust Company of Cuba buildings, their names still etched in stone above their monumental entryways. We walked by the stock exchange, and, eventually, made our way out into the Parque Central, situated at the border between intramural Havana and the modern city. Diagonally across from us stood the Asturian Center, built by Spanish immigrants at the end of the nineteenth century. Raul's grandfather had been one of its patrons. The city was dazzling that day. But it was clear that if Raul loved Havana for its architectural splendors, their main interest for him was not their intrinsic merit. The Centro Asturiano was not just an impressive *beaux-arts* building; it was an impressive *beaux-arts* building in Havana where Raul Rodriguez's Asturian grandfather had smoked cigars and talked of business and women. By the same token, the Palace of the Captains General was not just a very fine example of late Spanish colonial baroque, it was the finest *Cuban* example of that style and so of infinitely more interest to Raul than it would have been had he encountered it in Venezuela, say, or in Puerto Rico.

To have talked of architecture for architecture's sake, or history for history's sake, would have been to speak a foreign language—that of history, or architecture. And Raul, whatever the ostensible subject of his contemplation, was always speaking the same tongue: Cuban. The previous afternoon, we had gone to see the collection of Napoleonic memorabilia that the great Cuban sugar baron Julio Lobo had amassed and had brought to Havana in the late forties. We went through the museum painstakingly, past endless battle flags of the Grand Army, paintings of Murat and Ney, and cavalry swords that were as plentiful as stalks of sugarcane in Oriente Province. Raul had never evinced any interest in Napoleon before. And yet that day, no detail of the emperor's career was uninteresting to him. What counted, of course, was that this important collection was *in Havana*. Had he had the opportunity to view it in Paris, it is unlikely he would have taken the time. But that day, when he pointed to a plush settee, and said, "Look, that's the Empress Josephine's daybed," what he was pointing out was that his beloved Cuba possessed this piquant, distinguished object.

Cuba was the resting place of family bones and treasured memories. That much Raul and Ninon could know in Miami. But to return to Havana and to actually see the family crypt, or be confirmed in the idea that Miramar really was a beautiful neighborhood, was a way of keeping these memories fresh, at least if one had the stomach for the inevitable disappointments, the painful, desolating memories of what was not beautiful, what had not endured, that were part of the price of the ticket back. Moreover, the romance of Cuba had grown to such proportions during the decades of the exile that it was only later, after the visitors had gone back to Miami, that the real depression tended to sink in. While Raul was in Havana, it was as if he were high. Day after day, he would pursue his inspiriting round, though his wife's energy might flag and his son might grow increasingly mutinous, taking both a visual and a photographic inventory of the houses in which his and Ninon's friends and family in Miami had once lived. Actually, Raul had a sheet filled with these people's Havana street addresses folded up in his wallet, but after the first few days of the first trip, he found that he almost never needed to consult it. Instead, he would unerringly find the street in question, stop before a house, and, getting out of the car, walk over to it. Often, he found that he was only able to peer through the gates. So many of the houses of the exile bourgeoisie had been turned into embassies, schools, or government buildings. The house in Miramar in which Raul had spent several years, before the family had moved to the building now devoted to revolutionary botany, had been converted into a hospice for Nicaraguan soldiers mutilated during the Contra war. Invariably, Raul would take a photo; only then would he go back to the car. Sometimes, as he went, he would say to Ninon, "Well, we've done Carmen." At other times, he would seem lost in thought. And it was rare indeed for Raul to appear unsure of where he was, or what the building was that we were driving past. At those moments, in tones rich with anxiety, he would call out, "What was that, Ninon?" And she, for her part, would answer as best and as precisely as she could although once, as we neared the gate of the Cubanacan Country Club, instead of matter-of-factly giving the name, she found herself replying, "That was where I was so happy."

During each day, there was such a confusion of times and tenses. Every exile works on strange notions of time, ordering it—as it was perhaps never meant to be arranged—so that the past than the future take precedence over the present. That largely disused church in Miramar was a far more resonant sight to Raul than the sign the Cuban government had erected alongside it and that read, "Whatever Happens: Socialism!" And of course the shadow city of the Havana that might have been and that might yet be was inspiring in a way that the actual Havana could not possibly be. This did not mean that Raul, unlike so many of his fellow exiles who had never chosen to make the trip back to the city of their birth, imagined for one moment that those Cubans who actually lived in the houses his friends and family members had abandoned after the triumph of the revolution should be forced from them after Castro fell. That, he thought, was a recipe for civil war. But the knowledge that he could never have his house in Miramar back only made the opportunity to finally get a glimpse of these buildings for himself, and, just as importantly, to take back with him a visual record of the experience in the form of those precious carousels of slides, all the more essential.

What Raul had figured out was that it was only on this level that his Cuban past could be recaptured. Not for him the martial drums of political activism. If he was appalled by Fidel Castro, the politics of the Calle Ocho held no appeal for him either. And

Raul was skeptical about the chances of the leaders who dominated the Cuban exile scene ever playing an important role on the
island. "He who wins Eighth Street," he was fond of saying—
the formulation was the historian Luis Aguilar's—"loses Havana." And so, while the political debate flared on both sides of
the Strait, as Fidel Castro put his nation on war footing and a
hundred thousand Miamians signed petitions demanding that the
U.S. grant them the right to engage in a renewed attempt to
overthrow Communism on the island militarily, Raul kept returning to Havana, convinced that the only thing he could do was to
reinforce his memories with the refreshment of experience—no
matter how painful such exposure could be—so that, whatever
happened, he would have more of Cuba, even if he and his family
never left Miami, never returned to the island to live, than faded
dreams and hopes already doomed to disappointment.

That was why he was so adamant about going back to the
island as often as possible. When travel from Miami had been
barred in the aftershock of the Mariel boatlift, Raul had been
heartbroken. But before long, other events in his life came to
overshadow even such a cherished concern. There was the joy of
fatherhood (Ruly was born in 1979), and the overwhelming pain
of losing both his brother Alex and his father to violent death.
And, more prosaically, there was the need to make his way as an
architect. By 1990, however, Raul was as inured as he would
ever be to the losses he had suffered, and as established in his
profession as a small practitioner could realistically expect, which
was to say that he was both successful and insecure at once. He
was ready to go back. There were other encouraging congru-
ences. Ruly was eleven, the age Raul had been when he had left
Cuba. Ninon's professional career was going well. And the word
from Havana was that, finally, attitudes frozen for so long might
be on the verge of changing.

I had first met Raul and Ninon in 1986, through the good
offices of an English friend, while I was completing a book on
Miami. Raul had been immensely generous both with his time
and with contacts. But though he responded to my questions
about Miami with intelligence and indefatigable courtesy, it was

clear even then that the city he really wanted to talk about was Havana. He was still showing the slides of the 1980 trip to his friends, all the while wondering if he and Ninon would ever be allowed back to Havana again. To my surprise, shortly before I left Miami in the winter of 1987, Raul confided to me that he did plan to make a trip, and, to my surprise, asked if I would like to accompany him and his family. Slightly to his surprise, I think, I accepted. It was three and a half years before we actually did go, but, in July of 1990, I met the Rodriguezes at Miami International. They had the sounds of weeping family members still ringing in their ears, but their own nervousness was tinged with elation at finally getting to go back. We boarded the Haiti Trans Air flight and were off.

During that trip, Raul had been full of hope. Temperamentally, he was anything but a Don Quixote, nor was he possessed of any fantasy of himself as the man of destiny who would usher in a new era in the relations between the exiles and the Cubans of the island. Nonetheless, he arrived in Havana believing—this was, after all, before the final collapse of the Soviet Union—that by talking to Cubans who were loyal to the régime, in other words, to bureaucrats as much as if not more than to dissidents, and by demonstrating to them that not all Miami Cubans were the ogres they imagined from official propaganda, perhaps he might contribute to at least a reopening of communication. "We are each the sum of the other's fears," he would say, and, when he addressed his Havana interlocutors, insist that "respect and confidence, those are the first things that are required if Cubans are not to remain divided forever." He believed so strongly then that his generation—those who had not been old enough to fight the battles of the revolutionary period but still retained their passionate memories of life on the island—held the key to this national reconciliation. "Our parents are too old, and too compromised by their experiences," he kept saying, to whoever would listen to him, "and as for our children, though I wish that they felt otherwise, they don't care for Cuba as we do. Those of us who love our country must act, and act quickly."

Wherever he spoke, whether it was to his relatives, to whom

he must surely have seemed like Santa Claus, for all the gifts he brought from Miami, and the supplies he purchased at the diplomatic hard-currency stores after he arrived, or to the Castroite apparatchiks to whom, as neither a supporter of the Cuban-American National Foundation nor a member of one of the small left-wing exile splinter groups, he must have appeared as exotic as a bird of paradise, Raul's words were as eloquent and affecting as a great theatrical performance. Even the most jaded of his listeners could not fail to be moved by them, even if, in practical terms, they largely remained unpersuaded. "This is my country, you see," Raul would say, "I will always feel that way, whether people here, or my American friends in Miami, wish that I did or not. So you must be able to imagine how unbearable it is when I come here and the Cuban government treats me like a tourist. Ninon and I were in born in Havana, but we have to apply for a *visa!* And to make matters worse, when permission is granted to us, we are not even welcomed like foreigners the way you treat David or even my son, Ruly, who has only his American passport, but treated like second-class Cubans. I know that it makes you uncomfortable to see us as we really are, not monsters or people who wish you harm but people who love Cuba, just as you do, but that's the way it is."

But although a few of his interlocutors might, albeit guardedly, give Raul to understand that they agreed with him, and wished for nothing more than a renewal of the dialogue that had been aborted in 1980, it soon became clear that no change in either official or unofficial conduct would soon be forthcoming. That was in 1990. After the full effect of the withdrawal of Soviet subsidies to the Castro regime, and, shortly after that, the complete collapse of the Soviet Union itself, sank in, the positions of both most Miami exiles and, of course, of the Maximum Leader himself only hardened further. As Raul understood from the outset, there had always been a great psychological risk involved in making the trip. When he returned to Miami, he would find that he was bitterly depressed for some weeks. "It's what the psychiatrists used to call an abreaction," his friend Ramon Mestre had remarked knowingly at the time. "That's when you're taken back to the memory and sight of your original trauma.'' But before too long, it had become clear to Raul that these emotional risks were now accompanied by the virtual certainty that, in practical terms at least, there was nothing for even the best-intentioned of people to do. If Raul wanted to return again, he would have to do so in the name of some personal agenda, and in the full knowledge that the political outcome was out of his hands. He and Ninon might be traveling south, but, on either side of the Strait, by 1992, most of the ambient noise was as nobly intransigent as it could be.

That was when Raul began to talk less and less about the possibility of leading a life that included both Cuba and the United States and began to emphasize more what the trips themselves had come to mean to him. ''I know I've ripped off my scabs,'' he would say, ''and I don't claim that the choice is right for everyone. But while it's painful, I don't see that I have any other choice.'' What he understood, of course, was that, like the Cuban revolution itself, the exile had simply gone on too long. Other Cuban Miamians might continue to tell themselves that if, for example, world Jewry could have remained faithful to the idea of Zion during more than two thousand years of separation from it, Cubans could surely manage to adhere to their dream of return for what, even the gloomiest among them would concede, was a diaspora that was bound to end by the millennium. This Cuba that they loved was something almost as mystical as Israel, and, at the same time, far more concrete. It was a country that many in Miami had grown up in, and it was only a hundred and forty miles away. But it was precisely this set of seemingly irrefutable convictions that Raul, now that he had actually made another trip to Havana, had come to mistrust so thoroughly. If he was going to recover his past at all, he reasoned, he would have to do so in Havana now, before Castro fell but also before his son Ruly came into his American manhood.

Simply by watching Ruly, watching his American son explore the Havana he would never love as a native, Raul could see that the unitary, fixed idea of ethnic identity with which he and Ninon had grown up, and to which they still adhered, was

crumbling. Even in the Jewish case, it had been above all the
ghetto that had kept the dream of return alive through the cen-
turies—the ghetto, which was to say, persecution, and the Jewish faith itself—and even a nationalism as extreme as the Cuban
was not a faith with that kind of rootedness in history. Raul's
grandfather had only come to Cuba in the first decade of the
twentieth century. The whole Cuban period of the Rodriguez
family had lasted less than fifty years. It was absurd to talk of
Cuban Miami being a ghetto, or even to suppose that as a demographic and cultural enclave it would survive indefinitely.
There had been too many displacements already, and while the
Cubans of Miami might recoil from the idea that they were immigrants in America, the truth was they had quite recently been
immigrants to Cuba, and were, however unwillingly, far more
a part of the world of displacement and modernity than of the
premodern world of sun, soil, and community. *El exilio* might
mourn for the Cuba of the past, and continue to eye American
mores and the U.S. political establishment with frustration,
anxiety, and ambivalence, but it had come to think of Miami as
home, however unhappy that thought might appear from time
to time, and, especially, when the news from Cuba itself
seemed to presage change.

As he became a frequent visitor to the island, most of the
changes that Raul noticed were for the worse. The cigarettes that
had been available on one visit had disappeared by the next.
People grew visibly thinner, and the few private cars that were
still running disappeared, replaced by bicycles. In a practical
sense, the worsening economic situation on the island meant that
each trip cost Raul more money, which, with Miami mired in
recession, he could ill afford. His role was becoming to provide,
on a semiannual basis, a long list of necessities that his relatives
in Havana had no way of obtaining otherwise. "Our job is to help
people there," he said. "More and more that's our only job." No
trip was complete without Raul and Ninon being entrusted with
letters from friends in Havana to relatives in Miami. Almost
invariably, they were entreaties for help in getting out of Cuba.
One read:

Dear Uncle,

I need to write you of a most serious matter, of my *emigration* to the United States. I am a hard worker and in this country even hard work gets you nothing. I would not disgrace our name, and ask you to take my request to heart.

With an embrace to you, dear uncle, I remain your nephew.

[L.]

And another, from a middle-aged woman married to a lifelong revolutionary and now in despair:

Daddy dear,

It is hopeless here. I want to live with you. If [A.] comes, then so much the better. I have asked Raul to see what situation may be possible for him, but whatever happens I can bear it no longer. [L.] is desperate and I fear that there will never be anything for him here.

Your loving daughter,

[B.]

If Cuba had been for so long in the heart of Miami, then it appeared that Miami was increasingly in the heart of Havana. Whether, in fact, what was occurring was the political endgame remained unclear, but that people on both sides of the Strait were confronting both their oldest and most recent feelings, and plumbing the depths of these emotions they had lived with so long, was undeniable. The difference was that if in both Havana and Miami people dreamed of transformation, Raul was no longer certain about what he wanted and Ninon had abandoned hope. If anything, in 1991, she had been even more eager than Raul to return to Havana. Never having felt as comfortable in Miami as he had, she had dreamed that in Cuba she might finally come to rest in a place she could call home. "Cuba was my last chance," she told me later. "I kept imagining that I would find a place there, that at last there would be a country or at least a city where I would not feel *out* of place. But the more we got to know Havana, and spent time with the people there, the more I realized I didn't have anything in common with these people—nothing special in common with them, anyway—and that I didn't belong there either. I was a foreigner. Even though I was born in El Vedado, I was a foreigner.''

The conclusion that Ninon drew was unsparing. "It's just too late for us," she said. "Maybe we came to the United States as exiles rather than as immigrants, but after thirty-three years that fact turns out to make much less of a difference than I would ever have imagined or wanted. We Cubans have become a different people in America, and what I learned during our trips to Cuba is that they have become different down there as well." The tears began to well up in her eyes, and she shook her head angrily. "I don't care what anyone here thinks," she exclaimed, "the truth is that we are never going back! The only solution that I see now is for all of us to try to make the best of it. It's not that I don't love Cuba, but, as I said to Raul the other night, we have to think about other journeys, real and personal ones both. Maybe we should take Ruly to Madrid, or Rome, or Chicago. As for Cuba, I'm willing to return there once a year to take care of Raul's family, but aside from that we have to let go. There's nothing there for us in Havana anymore. And that seems so awful to me, as if we had been in mourning for nothing all these years, and loving a place that no longer exists except inside us.''

"And Ruly?" I asked.

"Oh, Ruly," she said, trying to smile. "He never cared very much. He tried to at first, out of love for us, but from the beginning I think he knew that we belonged in Miami, that this was home.''

I never saw Raul Rodriguez break down and weep, as Ninon did when the word "home" crossed her lips. As he himself admitted, this was because for a long time he refused to come to terms with the bad news. The inability of his wife and son to enthusiastically participate in subsequent trips to Havana confused and demoralized him at first. "The Cuban government made it difficult for me to go back," he told me late one night during this period, as we sat over *café cubano* at the Versailles, "but they didn't say I shouldn't go. Mas Canosa did not try to stop me. But Ninon and Ruly, the people I care most about in the world, don't want to go. My son was always the most important part of the trip in my eyes, but the other night, he told me that he hated Cuba, that he never wanted to go there again. And I tried to look at things the way he was doing—I know he can't see it the way I do—but I also found it to be hard to take, a lot harder than I expected.''

There was worse to come. In August of 1991, when we did go back, Ruly's reaction was to express even more estrangement from all things Cuban than either Raul or Ninon had anticipated. Believing that one of the things that had gone wrong the last time was that there had not been enough for the boy to do, they had timed the trip to coincide with the Pan-American Games that Cuba was scheduled to host that summer. Raul assured his son that they would get tickets for the U.S.-Cuba baseball game. He was true to his word, even though Ruly's full-throated rooting for the U.S. team (it included several players from South Florida) must have filled him with a volatile mixture of pride and regret. But after the game was over—to Ruly's chagrin, and his father's secret delight, the Cuban team won—Ruly was ready to go home. This boy who was never separated from his parents for more than a day, who was used to being driven to school by his father in the morning and being picked up at the school bus stop by his mother in the afternoon, volunteered that he would prefer to fly back to Miami the following day and stay with his grandparents until Raul and Ninon returned. This he said the evening of the game, as Raul, Ninon, my friend Ariane Zurcher, and I sat with him trying to convince him that five more days in Havana was not so long to be away from —there was no other word for it—home.

And if Ruly could not persuade his parents to let him leave, nor Ariane and I to return with him, neither could Raul and Ninon persuade him to eat. The following morning he began what Raul would later call his personal ''act of repudiation.'' Adamantly insisting that the food in Cuba was inedible—he was, even in Miami, an extremely finicky eater—Ruly survived for the rest of the trip on cheese balls and Tropicola—the Cuban version of Coca-Cola that had begun to be manufactured after the American bottler's plants had been expropriated by the revolution—bought in the hard-currency food shop of our hotel. Raul might insist that he had to eat, Ninon might implore him to eat, and Ariane and I might insist that the food was not so bad, but Ruly held his ground, and it was to the background music of this firm, implacable hunger strike that the rest of our time in Havana was spent.

At the time, father and son couldn't have been further apart, an uncomfortable position in as close-knit a family as the Rodriguezes. But in the end it was Raul who slowly began to edge closer to his son's position, and, certainly, further and further away from the attitudes that had informed the 1980 trip and the first 1990 visit. "My husband knows we can't go back to Cuba," Ninon told me, six months later. "He still struggles against it, but he knows. We have to look after ourselves here in Miami. Maybe, if the economy ever picks up, we'll start building a swimming pool, or make one of those other trips I keep talking about. Raul has already started an addition to the house." She giggled. "It's a new closet for me; he calls it the closet of Cheops. But even if we don't go anywhere or build anything, we have to learn to accept that this is home. I said to Raul the other day, 'We have each other, and Ruly, and we live here in Miami. We're never going back to Havana to live.' And do you know what, David?" She paused, savoring the moment. "He agreed with me!"

In the end, how could Raul have done otherwise? For all his passion for *el tema,* the golden memories of Cuba that he would carry in his heart until the day he died, he realized all great loves are mortal, if not in one generation or in one lifetime, then surely in the next. Rapt as he was by the sight of one of the great town houses along Paseo, it had not escaped Raul that while he was recapturing his lost city, Ruly had never left the United States, at least in his head. Under the fine trees of the boulevard, Ruly would run with complete insouciance. Sometimes, he would gesture impatiently at his parents to join him. But at other times, he would find himself lost in passions of his own. More than once,

Ruly would lift up his arms in imitation of a basketball player shooting a jump shot, leap into the air, and then, pumping his fist, shout to nobody in particular, "That's two points for Michael Jordan! Yes!" And, when he turned, there was an expression of triumph on his face almost as great as the satisfaction he exhibited, the day before we were due to leave for Miami at the end of the August trip, at the sandwich that he had eaten in a cafeteria in Miramar reserved for foreign diplomats and their families. "It's okay," he said between bites, "almost normal. The way it would be in Miami."

His father's epiphany, sadder and less welcome, would come the next day, when we touched down at Miami International Airport. It had been a difficult leave-taking in Havana, with relatives and friends pressing notes to be taken back to Florida into Raul and Ninon's hands. Inside the terminal building, the Cuban authorities were being particularly bloody-minded. At one point, a customs inspector told Raul that his passport was not in order, and he might be forbidden to leave. And though we were all eventually allowed to board the plane, we were all raw with anxiety. The thought of being asked hostile questions by U.S. Immigration inspectors as well seemed suddenly to loom like a tremendous obstacle. "Do you have all the American declarations?" Raul kept asking. And although Ninon kept assuring him that she did, his nervousness did not abate either on the plane or on the passport control line after we had landed.

The U.S. customs official on duty was a native-born American black in his late thirties. "Raul Rodriguez," he said, mispronouncing Raul's last name. "Rod-ri-gew-ez" was the way he said it. "Where are you coming from today, Raul?"

"Cuba," Raul answered, stiffening.

There was a pause. The officer said nothing, consulting his computer screen. Then he smiled broadly, stamped Raul's blue American passport, and said simply, "Welcome home, Raul."

And Raul Rodriguez realized then, to his sorrow, relief, and astonishment, that he really was home, exile though he would always consider himself to be, in the heart of Southwest Miami. The move had been made, the transplant had been effective, and Raul and Ninon Rodriguez and their son, Ruly, had become Americans after all. And whatever happened in Cuba, it was as Americans that their destinies and their dreams would be played out, as the millennium made its daunting, speedy approach.

Acknowledgments

SINCE ALL WRITING, but particularly the kind of non-fiction that laps at the borders of several genres that I tend to write, is both predatory and appropriative by its nature, my deepest thanks must go to Raul, Ninon, and Ruly Rodriguez. Both the adults, and, perhaps, the boy as well, must have known that there would be things I would write that would cause them pain, other things that would cause embarrassment, and, more generally, that to let a professional outsider into one's life is to sanction a portrait with which one is bound to find fault. Nonetheless, they invited me along for the ride—through Miami and Havana, through exile and also that ambiguous state of belonging that so many Cuban-Americans experience in the United States—or, come to think of it, the rides. And this book is as much the product of our dialogue over the course of the past three years as of anything they permitted me to observe or that I uncovered on my own.

Many others aided and abetted me along the way, but I would particularly like to thank Mitchell Kaplan and Julius Ser, the owners of Books and Books in Coral Gables, Florida, and those who work in that wonderful store, for their hospitality during the time I was researching this book. It is no exaggeration to say that without them, and the desk and the friendship that they provided me at some considerable inconvenience to themselves, this book might never have been written.

Index